MATTEO BRUNO
FOUNDER OF MELBOURNE'S MEATBALL AND WINE BARS

EPIC MEATBALLS

120 NEXT-LEVEL MEATBALL RECIPES
including recipes for
SIDES, SAUCES
and GARNISHES

murdoch books
Sydney | London

MEATBALLS

CONTENTS

I AM SORRY for WHAT I SAID
WHEN I WAS
Hungry
MEATBALL & WINE BAR

INTRODUCTION

Coming from a long line of cattle farmers, both in Italy and France, I have always recognised the importance of knowing where your food comes from. It was ingrained in me from birth. I am the youngest of four brothers, and dinner was always a massive undertaking for my mother, who would regularly prepare large sections of meat from the cattle my father would produce out on the farm. I remember going to the Perth Royal Show as a young child and seeing a prized steer win the blue ribbon. My father would always buy the prize winner for the family and we'd soon be enjoying enormous T-bone steaks for dinner. I suppose it was at the family kitchen table where my passion for food really began.

My profession as a film and television producer has given me the opportunity to explore topics of interest to me, and it's no surprise that in recent times all my work has been skewed towards producing food television. I've had the pleasure of filming with Australia's most celebrated chefs, and I've seen the passion and dedication required to make it to the top.

It was through the process of filming food programs that I was inspired to do something of my own – to open a restaurant in Melbourne, a city widely recognised as having one of the best and most diverse ranges of cuisine in the world.

But what would this restaurant be? It needed to be comfortable, affordable and incredibly tasty. It had to have meat. It had to be meatballs!

And, so, the first of my group of restaurants was born. It was Australia's first meatball restaurant – The Meatball & Wine Bar – in the dining precinct of Flinders Lane in Melbourne's CBD.

At the restaurant, I started experimenting with different types of proteins and aromatics to produce distinctive flavour and texture combinations. I worked closely with my butcher to determine which cuts of meat would produce the best result. It was more complicated than you would think: each protein reacts differently during the cooking process. In the restaurant game, a lot rides on consistency of product, so I had to test and re-test all my recipes so I could confidently produce the same result each and every time. I learned about the importance of keeping your minced (ground) meat nice and cool; cooking with a combination of heat and humidity; the appeal of fresh herbs and aromatics; the importance of texture across a spectrum of different meatballs; but, most importantly, I learned about what people liked and why.

This book features some of the recipes used in my three restaurants, which currently serve around 10,000 happy diners each week. I hope you will find joy in making these meatballs, and that the recipes you take from this book and develop into your own will stay with you and your family for generations to come.

Matteo Bruno

TOOLS OF THE TRADE

Soft hands

There are no better tools than your own hands to mix and roll meatballs. Use your fingers to combine and fold the meatball ingredients, and use your cupped hands to gently form the round meatballs. Not overworking the meat and keeping the pressure as light as possible will ensure your balls don't become rubbery or tough. And always clean and dry your hands thoroughly before working with them.

COLD FRIDGE

Keeping it cool is what making meatballs is all about. Your minced (ground) meat should be as cold as possible at all times. Most domestic fridges sit between 3°C (37°F) and 5°C (41°F), which is fine, but if you can cool your meat to 1–2°C (33.8–35.6°F) before mincing, you will not only get a better textured meatball, but the lifespan of your meat will be extended.

BONING KNIFE

A good boning knife can be used to break down joints of meat into the required cuts, or can be used as a finishing tool to trim the excess fat or connective tissue off a selected cut. Boning knives have a flexible blade, which can bend and follow the contours of bones, allowing you to remove the meat effectively.

MEAT GRINDER

It is fairly common these days for most domestic food processors to have meat mincing attachments and they work perfectly well in most applications, but for the more serious meatball aficionado, a dedicated meat mincer is required. They come in various sizes to suit all needs and are described in detail in the Minced Meat section (pp 10–11).

Mixing bowl

A wide, deep mixing bowl is a vital tool you need to prepare the perfect meatball. Use glass or metal bowls, if possible. Note that glass retains the temperature of ingredients a little better than metal.

Ice-cream scoop

Use an ice-cream scoop to ball up minced meat into consistent portions, about 50 g ($1^3/_4$ oz) each.

DIGITAL SCALES

Good-quality digital scales will allow you to measure individual portions of meatballs right down to the gram. You don't always have to be precise – after all, making meatballs is about having fun – but for those who want to be exact with their portions, digital scales are the way to go.

DIGITAL THERMOMETER

A digital thermometer is a must-have – especially if you're making large batches of meatballs that you may reheat down the track. As a guide, try to bring the centre of your meatballs up to 74°C (165°F); this temperature is hot enough to kill any potentially harmful bacteria. Avoid going much higher than this to ensure you don't dry out your meatballs.

Frying pan

A frying pan with a nice heavy base is ideal so there are no hot spots to burn your meatballs. Try to find a pan suitable for the oven as well, as many recipes start on the stovetop and finish in the oven.

BAKING TRAYS

A nice, high-sided baking tray is ideal for baking meatballs, and if you can find one that's non-stick on the base and sides, you're already ahead of the game. A bakers tray with indents is also perfect for baking meatballs. The divots are rounded, which hold the shape of your meatballs. You can turn the ball halfway through the cooking process to expose each side to the bakers tray so a nice crust can form.

OVEN

In a perfect world we'd all have combination ovens that cook with convection heat and controlled humidity. If you don't have one, add an ovenproof saucer of water inside your regular oven to create humidity. The wider your saucer, the higher the humidity level in the oven.

MINCED MEAT

Minced (ground) meat is the meatball's key ingredient. It's the very foundation of the meatball, so it's vital that you use the highest-quality meat you can find. We can get highly technical about minced meat and all the properties of each protein, but for the purpose of this book, we'll abide by four simple principles.

1. FRESH IS BEST

Always try to use the freshest minced meat you can find. Raw minced meat oxidises quite quickly, so try to reduce the time your minced meat is exposed to the air.

2. KEEP IT COOL

Raw minced meat warms quite easily, so try making your meatballs in a cool environment if possible. Keeping your minced meat cool will also help when shaping your meatballs so you can produce round and proud meatballs.

3. Treat it gently

The more you work the minced meat, the more you will agitate the proteins in the meat, which will naturally try to bind back together. By using soft hands and only working the minced meat to the absolute minimum, you'll ensure your meatballs are tender and delicate.

4. FAT IS YOUR FRIEND

We already know that fat is flavour, but in meatballs it's much more than that. It's moisture, which means texture – which means tasty meatballs!

KNOW YOUR BUTCHER

When it comes to making quality meatballs, your butcher is a key player in supplying you with the very best minced meat for the job. Be specific with your requests and you'll soon enjoy an enriched relationship where you'll gain access to the freshest, tastiest meats.

Butchers are likely to have amazing pieces of meat in the cool room, often secondary cuts of meat that are perfect for meatballs. Ask them if they have anything special this week – it might be a shoulder of veal, fresh lamb necks or some game meats, such as wild boar or venison. Your butcher can inspire your meatball experience, so that's the place to start.

Mincing your own meat

Mincing attachments are readily available for domestic food processors and it's a relatively inexpensive way to start experimenting with different proteins, which you can grind at varying levels of coarseness. But if you're serious about making meatballs, you'll want to invest in a meat mincer.

Meat mincers come in various sizes to suit all needs. When purchasing a dedicated meat mincer, there are three main things to consider: the cutting blade; the mincing plates (grinding plates); and the operating temperature of the machine.

The blade is the element that chops the meat as it passes through the funnel via a mixing worm. Blades need to be kept razor sharp. Make sure that when the blade rotates across the face of the mince plate, it does not touch or scrape against the mincing plate. This will rapidly dull the blade and can even shave tiny pieces of metal into your mince – not what you want!

The mince plate will give you the desired coarseness of mince. The finer the plate, the finer the minced meat will be. The bigger the plate, the coarser the minced meat will be. Using different plates at different stages can help you create the optimal texture for your meatballs. Some proteins, such as chicken, will bind very easily, so you won't need to mince them as finely. Others, such as pork, will need finer mincing if you're after a smooth consistency. You can use the large sized plates to combine different cuts of meat before passing them through a final mince plate of your desired coarseness. Generally, a safe go-to mince plate is the 3.5 mm plate. This will see you through most of your mincing requirements.

It's important that your minced meat stays as cool as possible at all times. If the motor of the mincer is too close to the mincer head, it will start to heat up, which will actually begin to cook your meat, reducing its lifespan. Keep your cuts of meat chilled before mincing to avoid this, and also keep the mincer head and all other attachments in a cool place (you can even keep them in the refrigerator before use).

ABOUT THE PROTEINS

We know that minced (ground) meat comes from larger cuts of meat that have been put through a meat mincer, but which cuts of meat produce the best minced meat? The answer is relatively simple: cuts of meat with a good proportion of fat in them tend to produce the best quality minced meat.

It's important to recognise what the word 'trimmings' means. Trimmings are offcuts of meat, the leftovers after a carcass has been deboned. They usually consist of some usable fat and meat, but can also include excessive sinew and connective tissue. Avoid trimmings where possible and opt for primary or secondary cuts of meat. Then, you'll know exactly what you're getting.

LAMB

Being a young animal, the lamb's meat is naturally tender and is a great carrier of flavour. Lamb tends to have softer and more delicate fat, which makes it perfect for minced meat in meatballs. If using mutton, you'll notice the meat will be darker than lamb. Mutton still produces good-quality minced meat, but it has a more pronounced flavour and the texture won't be as subtle as the meat you'll find in lamb. The following lamb cuts are ideal to experiment with in the kitchen.

SHOULDER: Wonderfully flavoursome, the shoulder of lamb makes perfect minced meat. It has a nice balance of meat and fat and as the muscle is relatively active, it's packed full of flavour. The benefit of using lamb is that most cuts are likely to be tender, and the shoulder is no exception.

LEG: Lamb leg tends to be leaner than other cuts and it should be used in combination with other fattier cuts of lamb. The leg produces excellent flavour and if you have the opportunity to debone a whole leg and mince it yourself, you'll find a range of different muscles in the leg – all with unique qualities, resulting in different types of minced meat.

BEEF

Minced meat from beef is the most common minced protein available. There are multiple cuts from this animal that make perfect minced meat for meatballs, and finding the combination suitable for your recipe is about trial and error. Opt for secondary cuts of beef, which have a good proportion of fat in them. These cuts are often cheaper to buy and result in the best meatball experience. Using a combination of cuts, minced at different levels of coarseness, can also be a way to experiment with your minced beef. The following cuts are some of the most suitable for mincing.

CHUCK: Chuck makes the perfect minced meat for meatballs as it has a great richness of flavour and balance of fat and muscle. This cut of meat comes from the shoulder of the animal. It gets a solid workout each time the cow lowers and raises its head to graze, making this cut darker in colour and full of flavour. The chuck has a high proportion of connective tissue and collagen, and requires fine mincing to reduce the risk of gristle in your meatballs.

INTERCOSTAL: This is the little finger of meat between the ribs and is one of the most flavoursome cuts you will find. It's full of fat and flavour but has a fair amount of connective tissue, which requires fine mincing. Using a portion of intercostal meat combined with other cuts of beef will result in a truly wonderful meatball experience.

SHIN: This cut of beef comes from the leg of the animal and is usually associated with osso bucco. The shin is a highly worked muscle, making it rich in flavour but also surrounded by lots of connective tissue. Shin will need to be minced fairly finely before use.

PORK

The secret behind using minced pork is the fat. Pork produces wonderful fat, which carries a load of flavour and moisture into your meatballs. Lean cuts, such as the loin, won't produce great meatballs as they don't have enough fat. However, you can combine these with other cuts to create the perfect textured meatball to suit your needs. The following pork cuts are worth considering.

SHOULDER: Pork shoulder contains a great ratio of fat, muscle and connective tissue, and is jammed full of flavour. You can add extra pork fat into the mix by using fat from the belly. Pork shoulder should see you through all your pork minced meat requirements.

LEG: As with other animals, the meat from the leg is comprised of many different muscles, some of which are close to the bone, making them extremely tasty. Leg meat has its fair share of connective tissue, which will break down when finely minced and slowly cooked. You may want to consider recipes that have other wet ingredients in them when using leg meat, as this meat tends to be drier than other cuts, such as the shoulder.

Chicken

Chicken thighs are always the best option when it comes to mincing chicken. The breast is too lean and will result in a rubbery and unenjoyable meatball, so it's best avoided. However, chicken livers and meat taken from anywhere besides the breast can be suitable for mincing. The same also applies to turkey and duck.

SEAFOOD

Although meatballs generally refer to dark meats, various types of seafood can be used for your meatball creations. Combinations of fish (just like combinations of meats) can make the most interesting fish meatballs. Generally speaking, firm, white-fleshed fish fillets will be suitable for making fish meatballs. Always ensure all bones and fish scales have been removed carefully before cooking your seafood meatballs. Squid, octopus, scallops, prawns and crustaceans of all varieties also make wonderful meatballs. As seafood is generally quite delicate, these balls may require a binding element to maintain their shape. Potatoes are a great ingredient for binding and they won't interfere with the delicate flavour profile of most seafoods.

COOKING TECHNIQUES

The recipes in this book call on several different cooking techniques, which have been selected to best suit each specific meatball recipe. Proteins react differently to different cooking styles. It's important to understand why this happens so you can choose the best cooking method to suit your needs.

A beef patty used in a hamburger, for example, is generally quite thin and can be made up of poorer-quality minced (ground) meat as the severe contact with a hot grill instantly melts away small pieces of gristle and fat while at the same time caramelising the surface of the patty. As most meatballs are too thick to be cooked purely via surface contact cooking, there's less room to hide, so the minced meat used for meatballs needs to be of the very highest quality.

Given the chance, most proteins will caramelise. Natural sugars in the meat will be drawn to the surface via contact with heat, and will produce a slightly sweet outer crust. This effect is often desirable for beef-based recipes. Other, more delicate proteins, such as pork or lamb, are usually better suited to gentle baking or poaching. Some proteins with less fat content, such as chicken or turkey, will require cooking methods where the humidity can be controlled so the meatballs don't dry out.

Some meatballs benefit from a combination of cooking techniques – for example, a wet meatball might benefit from a quick shallow-fry to seal the meatball before finishing the cooking in the oven. Or a more delicate meatball might require gentle poaching before searing it in a pan to give it a crust. Either way, use these cooking techniques as a guide, and know that there is one fallback method that can be used to create all of these meatballs – oven baking.

Baking meatballs in an oven has many advantages: the temperature is controlled; humidity can be manipulated simply by adding a saucer of water to the oven; cooking times can be easily monitored; and large batches of meatballs can be cooked at the same time.

Oven bake

By far the safest method for cooking your meatballs is to bake them in the oven. Humidity inside an oven is desirable if you are baking balls with little fat content, or if you want to bake large meatballs over a longer period without drying them out. Simply add an ovenproof saucer of water to the back of your conventional oven. The wider your saucer and the longer you keep it in the oven, the more humidity you will create. Conversely, keeping the oven free from moisture will enable you to form a nice crust on the exterior of your meatballs. Note that all ovens are different, and temperatures and conditions may vary, so always check that your meatballs are cooked all the way through after the suggested cooking time.

PAN-FRY

Cooking meatballs in a basic frying pan couldn't be simpler. Add a drizzle of olive oil to the pan and place on the stovetop over medium–high heat. Once the pan is hot, you can introduce the meatballs. Constantly move the pan in a circling motion, ensuring the balls cook evenly all the way around. Turning down the heat once the meatballs have taken on some colour is advised. Pan-frying meatballs is extremely effective for smaller meatballs, where the entire cooking can happen in the pan. As you increase the size of your meatballs, you can start by pan-frying them and then finish them off in the oven.

SHALLOW-FRY

This method is similar to pan-frying but involves cooking the meatballs in a larger quantity of oil (vegetable oil is perfectly suitable for this style of frying). Contact with hot oil creates a wonderful crust to the exterior of the meatball. By gently turning the meatballs over in the pan, you can fry all sides of the meatballs perfectly until the centre of the meatball is cooked. Shallow-frying works well with most meatballs and, in most cases, can be used to start or finish cooking meatballs.

Deep-fry

This method requires the full immersion of the meatballs into hot oil in a large saucepan. It's perfect for meatballs that require a rapid cooking time, such as liquid-filled meatballs or meatballs that require an outer crust. Some meatballs with delicate centres, such as seafood balls, often benefit from deep-frying as the outer crust that forms during frying helps to create texture in the meatball. Deep-frying is best done in small batches in vegetable oil and is a great method to use for meatballs that you wish to cook ahead of time and reheat later. Fill the saucepan just above halfway with oil and place over medium–high heat until the oil is approximately 160–180°C (315–350°F). You can test the temperature of the oil by dropping a small cube of bread into the oil. It's hot enough when the bread turns golden brown in 15 seconds.

GRILL

Exposing meat to an extremely hot surface to produce score marks can result in one of the very finest culinary experiences. This method is especially effective for meatballs with a high fat content, as the extra fat will keep the meatball moist during cooking. Smaller balls, made up of seafood such as prawns, also work particularly well with this cooking method.

STEAM

Steaming can be easily achieved at home with a steaming basket over a pot of boiling water, or by creating steam inside a paper bag by enclosing the meatballs in an envelope of baking paper and placing inside a humid oven – forming 'an oven within an oven'. This technique is referred to as *al cartoccio* in Italian and *en papillote* in French. Steaming meatballs is particularly effective when you're dealing with soft proteins, such as fish or crustaceans. Steaming is also effective on proteins like pork, but you will need to ensure that any meat you steam is minced extremely finely, as sinew or connective tissue tends to swell up during steaming.

Poach

Poaching your meatballs in some form of liquid (generally a tomato-based sauce) ensures they will remain juicy and tender. Poaching can be done on the stovetop over a gentle heat, or in the oven. Poaching meatballs is particularly effective when the poaching liquid is the sauce you'll be serving with the final meatball dish.

KEEPING IT SAFE

ALWAYS USE CLEAN SURFACES WHEN WORKING WITH RAW INGREDIENTS.

CLEAN YOUR HANDS THOROUGHLY BEFORE WORKING WITH MINCED MEAT.

TRY TO KEEP THE MINCED MEAT AND OTHER COOKING INGREDIENTS AS COLD AS POSSIBLE.

ALWAYS ENSURE THE MEATBALLS ARE COOKED ALL THE WAY THROUGH BEFORE EATING.

MEAT
DEPT.

MEATBALLS

This book explains how to prepare 60 different meatballs using a variety of meats and flavoursome ingredients. Most recipes use roughly 1 kg (2 lb 4 oz) of minced (ground) protein or primary vegetarian ingredient, which will produce around four generous portions. Adjust the recipes accordingly if you wish to create larger or smaller portions.

The recipes use a variety of cooking methods. Experiment with everything from poaching to grilling, and know that baking is a good fallback for almost every meatball featured in this book. Baking is a controlled cooking method in which a combination of temperature and humidity can be adjusted to suit all your meatball cooking needs.

Meat

Any meat can be minced at home using a domestic meat mincer; see Minced Meat (pp 10–11). However, this isn't necessary to produce wonderful, tasty meatballs. Regular store-bought minced meat will work perfectly well for all of these recipes, but I do recommend procuring your minced meat from a butcher wherever possible. Your butcher is likely to know more about where the meat came from and the meat is likely to be fresher and of better quality. Remember, when making meatballs, you'll need a good amount of fat, so avoid lean minced meat. If you're going to use chicken in your meatballs, make sure it's chicken thigh.

Many of these meatball recipes call on different types of proteins. This is because combinations of meats result in more interesting flavours and textures. You can be creative and customise the proportions of meats to adjust the recipes to your liking.

Technique

Make a test meatball before committing to cooking the entire batch. This gives you the opportunity to check the seasoning and make any flavour adjustments. Try to season as you go: season the minced meat and also the mixture associated with the recipe so when they combine, the flavours will be balanced and you'll get the very best result.

Once you've made a few meatballs, you'll begin to recognise that fairly wet mixtures produce the best meatballs. Don't be scared if the mixture is too wet to roll the meatballs. This can often be corrected by refrigerating the mixture for an hour, or by covering your hands in breadcrumbs when rolling. If you have time, refrigerate all meatball recipes to help the flavours develop. The raw meat (mixed or in ball shape) can be left covered in the refrigerator for a few hours for the aromatics to infuse into the proteins, making the meatballs even tastier.

Breadcrumbs

Breadcrumbs are used throughout these recipes and it's important to understand why we use them. In principle, breadcrumbs have two functions: 1) to retain moisture; and 2) to bind the meatball. By far the most important reason to use breadcrumbs is for moisture retention. The breadcrumbs soak up the cooking juices (fat included) and reduce the amount of moisture leaking out of the ball during cooking. But get the balance right – too many breadcrumbs will dry out your meatballs. You can use store-bought dry breadcrumbs, home-made breadcrumbs from dried old bread whizzed in a food processor, gluten-free breadcrumbs, fresh untoasted breadcrumbs, panko breadcrumbs (which are lighter and have crunch) and even milk-soaked bread to give a soft texture. Experiment with all these types of breadcrumbs and use your favourite kinds of breads to come up with your own version.

Sauce

When cooking meatballs in the oven, especially in large batches, you'll want to keep the leftover cooking juices. These are often highly aromatic and full of flavour. Transfer these cooking liquids to a pan with some stock, wine and butter, and then reduce them down by three-quarters to produce a wonderful sauce; or add them to a Chunky Italian red sauce (p 157) for extra depth.

The perfect combination

For a complete meatball dish, choose a meatball recipe, then choose a sotto palle (translation 'under balls', an accompaniment to serve with the meatballs) and decide on the sauce and garnish. With every meatball recipe, you will find a box listing some suggested combinations. The camera icon indicates the sotto palle, sauce and/or garnish shown in the photo. Use these suggestions as a guide only – feel free to combine any meatball with any sotto palle, sauce or garnish in this book.

CLASSIC BEEF

PAN-FRY / OVEN BAKE

MAKES 24 MEATBALLS

When using high-quality minced (ground) beef, the main flavour you're trying to achieve is beautiful, rich caramelised beef. This recipe uses 100% grass-fed beef and is enhanced by the use of simple accompanying herbs.

1 KG (2 LB 4 OZ) MINCED (GROUND) 100% GRASS-FED BEEF
10 ROSEMARY SPRIGS, LEAVES PICKED AND FINELY CHOPPED
2 TABLESPOONS DRIED OREGANO
6 GARLIC CLOVES, FINELY DICED
1 ONION, FINELY DICED
2 EGGS
40 G (1½ OZ/⅓ CUP) DRY BREADCRUMBS
175 G (6 OZ) CHUNKY ITALIAN RED SAUCE (P 157)
1 TEASPOON CHILLI FLAKES
30 G (1 OZ/1 SMALL BUNCH) FLAT-LEAF (ITALIAN) PARSLEY, LEAVES PICKED AND CHOPPED
35 G (1 OZ/⅓ CUP) FINELY GRATED PARMESAN CHEESE
OLIVE OIL, FOR FRYING

Add all of the ingredients into a mixing bowl and combine gently with your fingers. Gently roll the mixture into 60 g (2¼ oz) portions and set them aside.

Preheat the oven to 140°C (275°F).

Heat up a good drizzle of olive oil in an ovenproof frying pan over medium–high heat. Once the oil is hot, add the meatballs, taking care not to overcrowd the pan. You can do this in stages. Constantly move the pan in a circling motion. This will help the balls roll around and brown evenly. Do this for several minutes until the balls form a nice brown crust.

Once all meatballs are browned, add all the meatballs back into the frying pan and place in the dry oven for 12 minutes. This will complete the cooking process.

Serve while still hot.

Sotto palle

Creamy polenta (p 144) or
Lasagne sheets (p 146) or
Super potato smash (p 145)

Sauces

Chunky Italian red sauce (p 157) or
Red wine & beef stock sauce (p 163) or
Slow-cooked meat sauce (p 160)

Garnishes (pp 166-9)

Chilli oil or
Fresh herbs or
Grated cheese

MEATBALLS RUSTICO

POACH

MAKES 24 MEATBALLS

SUPER EASY TO MAKE AND INCREDIBLY VERSATILE, THESE DELICIOUS MEATBALLS CAN BE COMBINED WITH SPAGHETTI TO MAKE CLASSIC SPAGHETTI AND MEATBALLS, THEY CAN BE CRUSHED AND USED AS A TOPPING FOR PIZZAS, OR THEY CAN BE ENJOYED IN THEIR PUREST FORM WITH A LOAF OF CRUSTY BREAD.

- 400 G (14 OZ) MINCED (GROUND) PORK
- 300 G (10½ OZ) MINCED (GROUND) BEEF
- 300 G (10½ OZ) MINCED (GROUND) VEAL
- 4 SLICES WHITE BREAD
- 100 ML (3½ FL OZ) MILK
- 4 GARLIC CLOVES, FINELY CHOPPED
- 1 SMALL BROWN ONION, FINELY DICED
- 30 G (1 OZ/1 SMALL BUNCH) FLAT-LEAF (ITALIAN) PARSLEY, LEAVES PICKED AND FINELY CHOPPED
- 1 TEASPOON CHILLI FLAKES
- 2 TEASPOONS FRESHLY GRATED NUTMEG
- 50 G (1¾ OZ/½ CUP) FINELY GRATED PARMESAN CHEESE
- 160 G (5½ OZ/⅔ CUP) FRESH RICOTTA CHEESE
- 2 EGGS, PLUS 1 YOLK, LIGHTLY WHISKED
- 2 LITRES (70 FL OZ/8 CUPS) CHUNKY ITALIAN RED SAUCE (P 157)
- 50 G (1¾ OZ/1 LARGE BUNCH) BASIL, LEAVES PICKED AND TORN

In a mixing bowl, season the pork, beef and veal with salt and pepper. Soak the bread in the milk, then remove any excess milk by squeezing the bread in your hand. Tear up the bread into small pieces and add it to the meat.

Add the garlic and onion, parsley, chilli flakes, nutmeg, parmesan and ricotta cheese. Finally, add the egg to the meat mixture and fold everything together with your hands. Roll 60 g (2¼ oz) portions into balls and place them on a tray.

Pour the Red Sauce into a heavy-based saucepan over low heat and bring it to a gentle simmer. Tear up the basil leaves and add them to the sauce. Gently introduce the meatballs into the liquid one at a time, starting from the outside of the pot and working your way into the centre. Cook at a gentle simmer for 16–18 minutes. Once cooked, these meatballs should be tender and falling apart.

Sotto palle

Creamy polenta (p 144) or
Lasagne sheets (p 146) or
Cheesy bread (p 153)

Sauces

Chunky Italian red sauce (p 157) or
Italian veal jus (p 156) or
Napoli cruda (p 165)

Garnishes *(pp 166-9)*

Citrus zest or
Grated cheese or
Truffle salt

SELF-SAUCING BEEF JUS

OVEN BAKE

MAKES *20* MEATBALLS

WHEN YOU FIRST SLICE INTO THIS WONDERFUL BEEF JUS MEATBALL, A RICH, OOZING LIQUID SPILLS OUT FROM THE CENTRE, ESSENTIALLY SELF-SAUCING THE BALL. YOU CAN TRY THIS SAME METHOD WITH A LAMB BALL AND A MINT JELLY SAUCE IN THE CENTRE. IN FACT, THE IDEA BEHIND THIS STYLE OF MEATBALL CAN BE USED FOR JUST ABOUT ANY COMBINATION OF PROTEIN AND SAUCE MIX.

JUS

OLIVE OIL
1 KG (2 LB 4 OZ) BEEF BONES
1 ONION, COARSELY CHOPPED
LEFTOVER HERBS AND VEGETABLES
250 ML (9 FL OZ/1 CUP) RED WINE
1 LITRE (35 FL OZ/4 CUPS) BEEF STOCK
½ GELATINE SHEET (OR USE ⅓ TEASPOON GELATINE POWDER)

MEATBALLS

1 KG (2 LB 4 OZ) MINCED (GROUND) BEEF
100 G (3½ OZ/1 CUP) FINELY GRATED PECORINO CHEESE
1 ONION, FINELY DICED
3 EGGS
2 GARLIC CLOVES, FINELY DICED
2 TABLESPOONS OLIVE OIL
150 G (5½ OZ/1⅓ CUPS) DRY BREADCRUMBS
1 HANDFUL FLAT-LEAF (ITALIAN) PARSLEY, LEAVES PICKED AND CHOPPED
1 HANDFUL OREGANO, LEAVES PICKED AND CHOPPED
1 HANDFUL ROSEMARY, LEAVES PICKED AND CHOPPED
OLIVE OIL SPRAY, FOR BAKING

To make the jus, heat the olive oil in a heavy-based stockpot over high heat. When the oil's hot, add the beef bones. Turn the bones over until they have formed a deep brown crust on all sides.

Throw in the onion and any other vegetables and herbs you may have in the kitchen – these will all add flavour to the jus. Add the red wine and beef stock and stir them through. Turn the heat down to low and gently simmer, allowing the jus to reduce down to one-tenth of the original liquid. This will take around 2–3 hours.

Strain the liquid into a cup, dissolve the gelatine into it and stir through. Place in the refrigerator to cool and set. This will take around 1½ hours. Once set, the jus should be relatively firm to the touch.

Use a spoon to scoop out the jus in 5 g (⅛ oz) portions. Using your hands, gently roll the jus segments into balls, placing them on a tray. Put the balls into the freezer for at least 30 minutes.

To make the meatballs, season the beef with salt and pepper and fold in the remaining meatball ingredients. Mix thoroughly with your hands.

Preheat the oven to 160°C (315°F).

Form 70 g (2½ oz) balls and use your thumb to create a pocket in the centre of the meatball. Place a ball of the chilled jus inside, re-forming the meatball around it. Do this for all of the meatballs.

Spray a baking tray with olive oil and carefully place the meatballs in the tray. Bake in the dry oven for 12 minutes.

Remove from the heat and serve immediately. The centre of the balls should be melted and oozing with hot beef jus.

Sotto palle

Creamy polenta (p 144) or
Lasagne sheets (p 146) or
Super potato smash (p 145)

Sauces

Chunky Italian red sauce (p 157) or
Napoli cruda (p 165) or
Red wine & beef stock sauce (p 163)

Garnishes *(pp 166-9)*

Citrus zest or
Cracked black pepper or
Fresh red chilli

BEEF SHORT RIB MEATBALLS

MAKES *12* MEATBALLS

YOU CAN PUT ALMOST ANYTHING INTO A MEATBALL AND THIS RECIPE EXEMPLIFIES HOW EASY IT IS TO ADAPT SOME OF YOUR FAVOURITE DISHES. BEEF SHORT RIBS, WHEN COOKED SLOWLY IN A BRAISING LIQUID, ARE SOFT, UNCTUOUS AND DELICIOUS. BY FLAKING THE MEAT OF THE COOKED SHORT RIB, YOU CAN COMBINE IT WITH MINCED (GROUND) BEEF TO CREATE A BALL THAT CAN THEN BE COOKED USING ANY MEATBALL COOKING TECHNIQUE.

- 600 G (1 LB 5 OZ) BEEF SHORT RIB (THIN RIB), WITH BONE
- OLIVE OIL
- 1 ONION, SLICED
- 400 G (14 OZ) MINCED (GROUND) BEEF
- 1 FRESH RED CHILLI, DICED
- 30 G (1 OZ/¼ CUP) DRY BREADCRUMBS
- 1 EGG
- 2 HANDFULS (20 G/¾ OZ) FLAT-LEAF (ITALIAN) PARSLEY, LEAVES PICKED AND CHOPPED
- OLIVE OIL SPRAY, FOR BAKING

BRAISING LIQUID FOR THE SHORT RIB

- 1 CARROT, COARSELY CHOPPED
- 1 CELERY STALK, COARSELY CHOPPED
- 1 ONION, COARSELY CHOPPED
- 2 THYME SPRIGS
- 2 ROSEMARY SPRIGS
- 1 TABLESPOON DRIED OREGANO
- 1 TABLESPOON FENNEL SEEDS
- 500 ML (17 FL OZ/2 CUPS) RED WINE
- 500 ML (17 FL OZ/2 CUPS) VEAL STOCK (BUT ANY STOCK WILL DO)
- 4 DRIED BAY LEAVES

To prepare the beef short rib for cooking, season the meat with lots of salt and some cracked black pepper. In a deep heavy-set stockpot, heat up a drizzle of olive oil over high heat until it starts to smoke. Sear the short ribs until they form a deep crust on all sides. This should take 4–6 minutes. Remove the short ribs from the pot and set them aside.

To make the braising liquid, turn down the heat to low and add the carrot, celery, onion, thyme, rosemary, oregano and fennel seeds to the pot. Toss them around until they start to brown, then cover them with red wine. Place the short ribs back into the pot and top it up with stock until the ribs are covered. Add the bay leaves, then put the lid on the pot and let it cook gently for 4–6 hours, depending on the size of the ribs. You will know that they are fully cooked when the meat falls off the bone to the touch.

Once cooked, remove the short ribs from the pot, remove the rib bones and finely shred the meat with a fork into a bowl. You should have approximately 400 g (14 oz) of cooked meat. Strain the braising liquid and pour half of it over the shredded short rib meat before setting it aside to cool completely. Pour the other half of the strained liquid into a frying pan over low heat and simmer until it has reduced by half.

Caramelise the sliced onion by cooking it over low heat in a dry saucepan (with the lid on) until it turns a deep brown colour (about 20 minutes). Stir occasionally so the onion doesn't stick. Set aside to cool.

Preheat the oven to 180°C (350°F).

Remove the cooled short rib meat from the braising liquid and combine it in a mixing bowl with the now-cooled caramelised onion and the minced (ground) beef. Add the chilli, breadcrumbs, egg and parsley to the mixture and fold everything together with your hands. Form 80 g (2¾ oz) balls.

Spray a baking tray with olive oil and carefully place the meatballs in the tray. Bake in the dry oven for 8 minutes.

Heat up the reduced braising liquid in a pan over medium heat. Once bubbling, introduce the meatballs, moving them around gently so they are covered with the hot liquid and cook evenly. This will take around 8 minutes.

These delectable beef short rib meatballs are now ready to serve.

Sotto palle

Creamy polenta (p 144) or
Lasagne sheets (p 146) or
Super potato smash (p 145)

Sauces

Chunky Italian red sauce (p 157) or
Creamy mushroom sauce (p 164) or
Red wine & onion sauce (p 162)

Garnishes *(pp 166-9)*

Citrus zest or
Cracked black pepper or
Salt flakes

WAGYU BEEF

PAN-FRY
OVEN BAKE

MAKES 24 MEATBALLS

Minced (ground) Wagyu derives from the Wagyu breed of cattle, which is generally grain-fed, resulting in a rich and buttery meat, full of fat and flavour. This recipe respects the Wagyu by not adding many other ingredients into the meatball.

- 1 KG (2 LB 4 OZ) MINCED (GROUND) WAGYU BEEF
- 50 G (1¾ OZ) GHEE
- ½ BROWN ONION, FINELY DICED
- 1 EGG, WHISKED
- 80 G (2¾ OZ/⅔ CUP) DRY BREADCRUMBS
- 25 G (1 OZ/¼ CUP) FINELY GRATED PARMESAN CHEESE
- 100 G (3½ OZ) CHUNKY ITALIAN RED SAUCE (P 157)
- 2 GARLIC CLOVES, FINELY DICED
- 30 G (1 OZ/1 SMALL BUNCH) FLAT-LEAF (ITALIAN) PARSLEY, LEAVES PICKED AND FINELY CHOPPED
- 1 TEASPOON DRIED OREGANO
- ½ TEASPOON CHILLI FLAKES
- SALT FLAKES
- OLIVE OIL
- OLIVE OIL SPRAY, FOR BAKING

In a mixing bowl, season the Wagyu beef with salt and pepper. Add the ghee, onion, egg, breadcrumbs, parmesan cheese, red sauce, garlic, parsley, oregano and chilli flakes, and gently fold everything together using your hands. Roll the mixture into 60 g (2¼ oz) balls and set them aside to cool in the refrigerator for 30 minutes.

Once cooled, crack some salt flakes onto each ball; the salt will draw moisture and enable a crust to form on the meatballs when they hit the hot pan.

Preheat the oven to 120°C (235°F).

Heat up a good drizzle of olive oil in the frying pan over medium–high heat and add the meatballs, constantly moving the pan in a circling motion. This will help the balls roll around the pan and brown evenly. Do this for several minutes until the balls form a nice brown crust.

Spray the baking tray with olive oil and carefully place the meatballs in the tray. Finish the cooking in the dry oven for 8–10 minutes.

Serve immediately.

Sotto palle

Buttered edamame (p 147) or
Creamy polenta (p 144) or
Simple mushroom risotto (p 149)

Sauces

Barbecue sauce (p 161) or
Chunky Italian red sauce (p 157) or
Red wine & beef stock sauce (p 163)

Garnishes *(pp 166-9)*

Chilli oil or
Hazelnut pangrattato or
Micro herbs

LEAN BEEF & VEGETABLE

PAN-FRY
OVEN BAKE

MAKES 50 MEATBALLS

WONDERFULLY TASTY AND HEALTHY, THIS MEATBALL RECIPE CAN BE ADAPTED TO USE ANY OF YOUR LEFTOVER VEGETABLES. SIMPLY BLITZ THEM IN A FOOD PROCESSOR, COOK THEM IN A PAN AND ADD THEM TO YOUR PREFERRED MEAT AND YOU'VE CREATED A ONE-OFF MEATBALL THAT NOT ONLY MAKES GOOD USE OF YOUR FRIDGE LEFTOVERS BUT TASTES DELICIOUS!

- 1 CARROT
- 1 CELERY STALK
- ½ WHITE ONION
- 1 ZUCCHINI (COURGETTE)
- 4 GARLIC CLOVES
- ½ FRESH RED CHILLI
- 50 G (1¾ OZ/1 LARGE BUNCH) FLAT-LEAF (ITALIAN) PARSLEY, LEAVES PICKED
- 4 ROSEMARY SPRIGS, LEAVES PICKED
- 1 HANDFUL THYME, LEAVES PICKED
- 2 TEASPOONS FINELY GRATED NUTMEG, PLUS EXTRA FOR SEASONING
- 100 ML (3½ FL OZ) OLIVE OIL
- 125 ML (4 FL OZ/½ CUP) WHITE WINE
- 80 G (2¾ OZ) DRY BREADCRUMBS
- 750 G (1 LB 10 OZ) MINCED (GROUND) BEEF
- 2 EGGS, WHISKED
- 35 G (1¼ OZ/⅓ CUP) FINELY GRATED PARMESAN CHEESE

Start by adding all of the vegetables, the garlic, chilli, herbs and nutmeg into a food processor and blitzing into a very finely chopped mixture.

Add about 2½ tablespoons of olive oil to a frying pan over low heat and gently simmer the vegetable mix for several minutes. Add the white wine and continue to simmer for several minutes until all the vegetables are cooked. Add the breadcrumbs to the pan to absorb any residual liquid. Set this aside to cool.

Season the beef with salt and pepper in a mixing bowl. Add the eggs and parmesan cheese, and the cooled vegetable mix. Gently combine and roll the mixture into 30 g (1 oz) balls.

Preheat the oven to 160°C (315°F).

Heat up about 2½ tablespoons of olive oil in an ovenproof frying pan over a medium–high heat. Once the oil is hot, add the meatballs, taking care not to overcrowd the pan. You can do this in stages. Constantly move the pan in a circling motion. This will help the balls roll around the pan and brown evenly. Do this for 2–3 minutes until the balls form a nice brown crust.

Once completed, add all the meatballs back into the frying pan and place in the dry oven for 6 minutes. This will complete the cooking process.

Sprinkle some finely grated nutmeg over the balls before serving.

Sotto palle

Creamy polenta (p 144) or
Grilled mushrooms with taleggio cheese (p 150) or
Basic peperonata (p 151)

Sauces

Chunky Italian red sauce (p 157) or
Green sauce (p 164) or
Sofritto (p 159)

Garnishes (pp 166-9)

Chilli oil or
Fresh herbs or
Pickled zucchini

LE CREUSET
LE CREUSET

BONE MARROW

OVEN BAKE

MAKES **20** MEATBALLS

LIKE A HIDDEN JEWEL, BONE MARROW IS FOUND INSIDE THE SHINBONE OF A COW. IT'S GELATINOUS AND PACKED FULL OF FLAVOUR. IN THIS DISH, THE MARROW IS INSERTED INTO THE CENTRE OF THE BEEF BALLS SO THAT THE MEATBALLS TAKE ON THE MARROW FLAVOUR FROM THE INSIDE OUT. USE BEEF SHIN (SHANK) AS YOUR MINCED (GROUND) MEAT TO EXPERIENCE THIS RECIPE AT ITS FULL POTENTIAL.

- 120 G (4¼ OZ) BONE MARROW, CUT INTO 5–8 G (⅛–¼ OZ) SEGMENTS
- SALT FLAKES
- 1 KG (2 LB 4 OZ) MINCED (GROUND) BEEF
- 90 G (3¼ OZ) FINELY GRATED PECORINO CHEESE
- 40 SMALL CAPERS, RINSED
- ½ RED ONION, FINELY DICED
- 3 GARLIC CLOVES, FINELY DICED
- 80 ML (2½ FL OZ/⅓ CUP) CHUNKY ITALIAN RED SAUCE (P 157)
- 50 G (1¾ OZ/1 LARGE BUNCH) FLAT-LEAF (ITALIAN) PARSLEY, LEAVES PICKED AND COARSELY CHOPPED
- 150 G (5½ OZ/1⅓ CUPS) DRY BREADCRUMBS
- 3 SMALL EGGS
- OLIVE OIL
- OLIVE OIL SPRAY, FOR BAKING

Preheat the oven to 160°C (315°F).

Prepare the bone marrow by rolling the segments into balls and seasoning each of them with generous amounts of cracked black pepper and some salt flakes. Place the bone marrow balls onto a tray and into the freezer so they keep their shape.

To make the beef balls, combine the meat, pecorino cheese, capers, onion, garlic, Red Sauce, parsley, breadcrumbs, eggs and a good drizzle of olive oil in a large bowl. Use your hands to mix everything together. With this particular meatball, it's okay to work the mixture a little more than you normally would as you're trying to create a firmer outer section of the ball so that the marrow stays in the middle. Roll the mixture into 80 g (2¾ oz) balls. Take the bone marrow balls and push one into the centre of each meatball, re-forming the meatballs around the bone marrow.

Spray a baking tray with olive oil and carefully place the meatballs in the tray. Bake in the dry oven for 12 minutes and serve immediately. The centre of the meatballs should be gelatinous and oozing with delicious bone marrow.

Note: Ask your butcher for horizontal 'pucks' (or segments) of bone marrow, or you can scoop out the marrow from a vertically cut bone and shape it yourself.

Sotto palle

Creamy polenta (p 144) or
Lasagne sheets (p 146) or
Super potato smash (p 145)

Sauces

Chunky Italian red sauce (p 157) or
Red wine & beef stock sauce (p 163) or
Red wine & onion sauce (p 162)

Garnishes *(pp 166-9)*

Citrus zest or
Fresh herbs or
Prosciutto crisps

BEEF & VEAL WITH CHILLI-STUFFED OLIVES

SHALLOW-FRY
OVEN BAKE

MAKES *28* MEATBALLS

AN EASY GO-TO RECIPE FOR CHILLI LOVERS, THESE TASTY MEATBALLS MATCH BEEF AND VEAL WITH CHILLI-STUFFED OLIVES TO CREATE A WONDERFUL BALANCE OF FLAVOUR, TEXTURE AND HEAT.

- 200 G (7 OZ) STALE BREAD SLICES
- 250 ML (9 FL OZ/1 CUP) MILK
- 28 BLACK OLIVES
- 2 LARGE RED CHILLIES, SEEDED AND THICKLY SLICED
- 500 G (1 LB 2 OZ) MINCED (GROUND) BEEF
- 300 G (10½ OZ) MINCED (GROUND) VEAL
- 2 EGGS, WHISKED
- 100 G (3½ OZ/1 CUP) FINELY GRATED PARMESAN CHEESE
- 2 GARLIC CLOVES, FINELY DICED
- 1 TEASPOON CHILLI FLAKES
- 1 TABLESPOON PICKED ROSEMARY, FINELY CHOPPED
- 2 HANDFULS (20 G/¾ OZ) FLAT-LEAF (ITALIAN) PARSLEY, LEAVES PICKED AND FINELY CHOPPED
- 1 TABLESPOON FINELY CHOPPED SAGE
- 1 TEASPOON PICKED OREGANO
- 60 G (2¼ OZ/½ CUP) DRY BREADCRUMBS, FOR COATING
- OLIVE OIL, FOR FRYING

Soak the bread in the milk for several minutes, then squeeze out the excess milk and tear up the bread into small pieces.

Remove the pits from the olives and insert a slice of red chilli into each.

In a mixing bowl, season the beef and veal with salt and pepper. Add the egg, parmesan cheese, garlic, chilli flakes and herbs, and combine thoroughly. Roll the mixture into 50 g (1¾ oz) balls and insert a chilli-stuffed olive into each ball, re-shaping the ball around the olive. Roll the balls in breadcrumbs to completely coat.

Preheat the oven to 160°C (315°F).

Pour some olive oil into a deep frying pan until it's approximately 1–3 cm (½–1¼ in) deep, and place over medium–high heat. Introduce the meatballs a few at a time. They should start to sizzle on contact. Shallow-fry the meatballs for around 2–3 minutes on one side before turning them over to cook on the other side for 2–3 minutes. This will form a nice brown crust around the entire meatball.

Remove the meatballs from the oil and strain on paper towel. Spray a baking tray with olive oil and carefully place the meatballs into the tray.

Bake in the dry oven for 6 minutes.

Serve immediately.

Sotto palle

Cheesy bread (p 153) or
Creamy polenta (p 144) or
Simple mushroom risotto (p 149)

Sauces

Butter & sage sauce (p 159) or
Italian veal jus (p 156) or
Sofritto (p 159)

Garnishes (pp 166-9)

Fresh herbs or
Fresh red chilli or
Fried sage

BEEF, PEA & ZUCCHINI

MAKES *38* MEATBALLS

BASIC AND FOOLPROOF, THIS EXCELLENT BEEF BALL RECIPE WORKS EVERY TIME. IT CAN BE MADE IN ADVANCE AND SERVED DAYS LATER BY REHEATING THE COOKED MEATBALLS IN A BAKING TRAY IN THE OVEN COVERED IN FOIL. THE GRATED ZUCCHINI KEEPS THE MOISTURE IN THE MEATBALL – TRY USING IT IN OTHER RECIPES FOR THE SAME EFFECT.

150 G (5½ OZ) FROZEN BABY PEAS
ICE CUBES
1 KG (2 LB 4 OZ) MINCED (GROUND) BEEF
2 SMALL ZUCCHINI (COURGETTES), GRATED
125 G (4½ OZ/1¼ CUPS) FINELY GRATED PARMESAN CHEESE
½ WHITE ONION, FINELY DICED
30 G (1 OZ/1 SMALL BUNCH) FLAT-LEAF (ITALIAN) PARSLEY, LEAVES PICKED AND CHOPPED
2 TEASPOONS FRESHLY GRATED NUTMEG
1 WHOLE EGG, PLUS 1 EGG YOLK
VEGETABLE OIL, FOR FRYING
OLIVE OIL SPRAY, FOR BAKING

Cook the peas in lightly salted boiling water in a saucepan over high heat for about 5 minutes, or until the peas are cooked and tender. Then place them into an ice bath to stop them cooking.

In a large mixing bowl, season the beef with salt and pepper. Use your hands to combine the beef with all the remaining ingredients (including the chilled peas). Roll the mixture into 50 g (1¾ oz) balls and place on a tray. Set the balls aside to cool in the refrigerator for 30 minutes.

Preheat the oven to 180°C (350°F).

Pour some vegetable oil into a deep frying pan until it's approximately 1–3 cm (½–1¼ in) deep, and place over medium–high heat. Introduce the meatballs a few at a time. They should start to sizzle on contact. Cook the meatballs on one side for around 3–4 minutes before rolling them over to the other side to cook for another 3–4 minutes. This will form a nice brown crust around the entire meatball.

Remove the meatballs from the oil and strain on paper towel. Spray a baking tray with olive oil and carefully place the meatballs in the tray. Bake in the dry oven for 8 minutes.

Serve immediately.

Sotto palle

Basic peperonata (p 151) or
Buttered risoni & peas (p 144) or
Pea, mint & ricotta salad (p 147)

Sauces

Chunky Italian red sauce (p 157) or
Roasted capsicum sauce (p 158) or
Sofritto (p 159)

Garnishes *(pp 166-9)*

Fried sage or
Pickled zucchini or
Toasted pistachios

BEEF & PORK WITH LICORICE & RED WINE

OVEN BAKE

MAKES *20* MEATBALLS

THE STRONG FLAVOUR OF THESE MEATBALLS COMES FROM THE LICORICE AND RED WINE REDUCTION. YOU CAN USE THIS TECHNIQUE TO CREATE ANY VARIATION BY MAKING YOUR FAVOURITE REDUCTION AND INTRODUCING IT TO THE MINCED (GROUND) MEAT.

- OLIVE OIL
- 1 SMALL CARROT, COARSELY CHOPPED
- 1 CELERY STALK, COARSELY CHOPPED
- ½ SMALL ONION, COARSELY CHOPPED
- 2 DRIED BAY LEAVES
- 2 ROSEMARY SPRIGS
- 2 THYME SPRIGS
- 250 ML (9 FL OZ/1 CUP) RED WINE
- 200 ML (7 FL OZ) BEEF STOCK
- 1 FRESH RED CHILLI, FINELY CHOPPED
- 120 G (4¼ OZ) SOFT LICORICE, CHOPPED
- 20 G (¾ OZ) BUTTER
- 500 G (1 LB 2 OZ) MINCED (GROUND) BEEF
- 500 G (1 LB 2 OZ) MINCED (GROUND) PORK
- 30 G (1 OZ/1 SMALL BUNCH) FLAT-LEAF (ITALIAN) PARSLEY, LEAVES PICKED AND CHOPPED
- 2 GARLIC CLOVES, CRUSHED
- 50 G (1¾ OZ/½ CUP) FINELY GRATED PARMESAN CHEESE
- 80 G (2¾ OZ/⅔ CUP) DRY BREADCRUMBS
- OLIVE OIL SPRAY, FOR BAKING

Create the licorice reduction by pouring a good drizzle of olive oil in a heavy-set stockpot over medium–high heat. Add the carrot, celery and onion with the bay leaves, rosemary, thyme and a pinch of salt and pepper, and cook until you've given colour to the vegetables. Add the red wine, beef stock, chilli and the licorice pieces. Let this simmer and reduce by half. This should take around 90 minutes. By this stage, the licorice should have melted and the liquid will be viscous and full of flavour.

Strain the liquid, add a knob of butter and mix it through. You want to have around 200 ml (7 fl oz) of liquid at the end (keep a little extra aside for glazing the meatballs). Set this aside to cool.

Preheat the oven to 160°C (315°F) and add a small ovenproof saucer of water to the back of the oven to create humidity.

For the meatballs, season the minced (ground) meats with salt and pepper, then add the parsley, garlic, parmesan cheese, breadcrumbs and most of the cooled licorice reduction. Combine well and roll the mixture into 60 g (2¼ oz) balls.

Spray an indented bakers tray with olive oil. Using the excess licorice liquid, coat the balls, then carefully place them in the tray. Bake in the humid oven for 14 minutes.

Serve while hot.

Sotto palle

Creamy polenta (p 144) or
Super potato smash (p 145) or
Lasagne sheets (p 146)

Sauces

Red wine & beef stock sauce (p 163) or
Red wine & onion sauce (p 162) or
Roasted capsicum sauce (p 158)

Garnishes *(pp 166-9)*

Cracked black pepper or
Edible flowers or
Grated cheese

BEEF & SPINACH

MAKES *26* MEATBALLS

SPINACH AND BEEF ARE A WONDERFUL MATCH – AND WHEN PAIRED IN A MEATBALL, THEY OFFER ONE OF THE JUICIEST, TASTIEST COMBINATIONS YOU'LL EVER EXPERIENCE. YOU CAN USE EXTRA-LEAN BEEF FOR AN EVEN HEALTHIER OPTION. THESE MEATBALLS WILL REMAIN JUICY FOR DAYS, AND CAN BE EATEN HOT OR COLD.

- OLIVE OIL
- 300 G (10½ OZ) BABY ENGLISH SPINACH LEAVES
- ZEST OF ½ LEMON
- 3 GARLIC CLOVES, FINELY DICED
- 55 G (2 OZ/½ CUP) DRY BREADCRUMBS
- 500 G (1 LB 2 OZ) MINCED (GROUND) BEEF
- 1 EGG
- 50 G (1¾ OZ/1 LARGE BUNCH) FLAT-LEAF (ITALIAN) PARSLEY, LEAVES PICKED AND CHOPPED
- 1 TEASPOON FRESHLY GRATED NUTMEG
- 35 G (1¼ OZ/⅓ CUP) FINELY GRATED PARMESAN CHEESE
- PLAIN (ALL-PURPOSE) FLOUR, FOR COATING
- VEGETABLE OIL, FOR FRYING
- OLIVE OIL SPRAY, FOR BAKING

Pour a small drizzle of olive oil into a large frying pan over medium heat and add the spinach, the lemon zest and garlic. After a few minutes, when the spinach begins to break down and release moisture, add the breadcrumbs to absorb the juices. Continue to cook for around 5 minutes.

Remove the spinach mix from the pan and set aside in a bowl. Once it has cooled, finely chop it with a knife.

In a mixing bowl, season the beef with salt and pepper. Add the egg, parsley, nutmeg, parmesan cheese and the cooled and chopped spinach mixture, and gently combine. Form the mixture into 40 g (1½ oz) balls and roll them in the flour to coat.

Preheat the oven to 125°C (250°F) and add a small ovenproof saucer of water to the back of the oven to create humidity.

Pour some vegetable oil into a deep frying pan until it's approximately 1–3 cm (½–1¼ in) deep, and place over medium–high heat. Introduce the meatballs a few at a time. They should start to sizzle on contact. Cook the meatballs on one side for around 2 minutes before rolling them over to the other side to cook for another 2 minutes. This will form a nice brown crust around the entire meatball.

Remove the meatballs from the oil and strain on paper towel. Spray a baking tray with olive oil and carefully place the meatballs in the tray. Bake in the humid oven for 6 minutes.

Serve immediately.

Sotto palle

Buttered edamame (p 147) or
Buttered risoni & peas (p 144) or
Italian beans (p 154)

Sauces

Green sauce (p 164) or
Napoli cruda (p 165) or
Sofritto (p 159)

Garnishes *(pp 166-9)*

Grated cheese or
Herb oil or
Micro herbs

SEARED BEEF CARPACCIO

PAN-SEAR

MAKES 25 MEATBALLS

A SPHERICAL TAKE ON A CLASSIC BEEF CARPACCIO, THIS DELECTABLE MEATBALL MAKES THE PERFECT CANAPÉ – TO BE SERVED ON ITS OWN OR WITH A SAUCE. AS WITH ANYTHING YOU EAT THAT'S RAW, ENSURE YOU USE THE VERY FINEST INGREDIENTS YOU CAN FIND. THIS MEATBALL IS BEST ENJOYED SLIGHTLY CHILLED OR AT ROOM TEMPERATURE.

300 G (10½ OZ) BEEF FILLET
SALT FLAKES
EXTRA VIRGIN OLIVE OIL, FOR COATING
2 TABLESPOONS FINELY GRATED PARMESAN CHEESE
½ GARLIC CLOVE, FINELY DICED
1 TEASPOON EXTRA VIRGIN OLIVE OIL
20 CAPERS, ABOUT 6 G (⅛ OZ), RINSED AND FINELY CHOPPED
JUICE OF ½ SMALL LEMON
4 ROSEMARY SPRIGS, LEAVES PICKED AND FINELY CHOPPED
EGG YOLK (OPTIONAL)
RADISH, FINELY GRATED, TO GARNISH (OPTIONAL)

WASABI CREAM

1 TEASPOON SOUR CREAM
½ TEASPOON DIJON MUSTARD
½ TEASPOON WASABI PASTE

Season the beef fillet generously with salt flakes and cracked black pepper, and rub some olive oil over the beef. In a very hot frying pan, sear the meat on all sides for around 30 seconds over high heat or until it's a deep brown colour. Remove from the heat and set aside on paper towel to cool.

To make the wasabi cream, simply whisk together the sour cream, dijon mustard and wasabi paste until it forms a light cream.

Once the beef fillet has cooled, dice it finely with a sharp knife and season it again with salt and pepper. Combine the beef with the wasabi cream and the remaining ingredients in a large bowl. Place the mixture on a sheet of plastic wrap and roll it into a tight sausage. Place the sausage into the refrigerator to set.

After approximately 1 hour, remove the sausage from the refrigerator. Use a sharp knife to cut it into small sections and roll these into 15 g (½ oz) balls. You may want to cover your hands in olive oil while rolling to give the balls some additional gloss. They are now ready to eat.

Optional extras: Add a raw egg yolk to the mix for an extra creamy texture and garnish the balls with finely grated radish to finish.

Note: The simple wasabi cream in this recipe is well worth the effort. However, you can use 2 teaspoons of horseradish cream (p 162) or the store-bought variety instead.

Sauces

Aioli (p 160) or
Barbecue sauce (p 161) or
Spicy hoisin sauce with ginger & garlic (p 163)

Garnishes (pp 166-9)

Micro herbs 📷 *or*
Parmesan crisps or
Salt flakes 📷

RED DEVIL MEATBALLS

MAKES *50* MEATBALLS

THE RED DEVIL IS FOR LOVERS OF HEAT! THE BASE TO THIS RECIPE IS A SIMPLE BEEF BALL, WHICH HAS BEEN SUPERCHARGED WITH RED CHILLI. THERE'S A COOLING SURPRISE IN THE MIDDLE OF EACH BALL IN THE FORM OF A CREAM CHEESE CENTRE.

- 1½ TABLESPOONS CREAM CHEESE
- 2 TEASPOONS DIJON MUSTARD
- 1 KG (2 LB 4 OZ) MINCED (GROUND) BEEF
- 4–6 FRESH BIRD'S EYE CHILLIES, WITH SEEDS AND FINELY DICED
- 1 TABLESPOON DRIED OREGANO
- 2 EGGS
- 2 GARLIC CLOVES, CRUSHED
- 3 HEAPED TABLESPOONS DRY BREADCRUMBS
- 160 ML (5¼ FL OZ) CHUNKY ITALIAN RED SAUCE (P 157)
- 50 G (1¾ OZ/1 LARGE BUNCH) FLAT-LEAF (ITALIAN) PARSLEY, LEAVES PICKED AND CHOPPED
- 60 G (2¼ OZ) FINELY GRATED PARMESAN CHEESE
- 1 TABLESPOON OLIVE OIL
- OLIVE OIL SPRAY, FOR BAKING

Combine the cream cheese and mustard thoroughly in a mixing bowl, and then roll the mixture into small marble-sized balls. Carefully place them on a tray and into the freezer to set.

Preheat the oven to 200°C (400°F).

Combine all of the other ingredients together in a mixing bowl and season well with salt and pepper. Roll the mixture into 30 g (1 oz) balls. Insert the frozen cheese balls into the beef balls by creating a cavity inside the meatball with your thumb. Re-form the meatball around the cheese. Repeat until all the meatballs have a cheese ball in the centre.

Spray a baking tray with olive oil and carefully place the meatballs in the tray. Bake in the dry oven for 6–8 minutes.

Take the meatballs out of the oven and rest for 2 minutes before serving. The cream cheese centre should be warm and provide some relief from the fiery outer meatball layer.

Sotto palle

Creamy polenta (p 144) or
Lasagne sheets (p 146) or
Super potato smash (p 145)

Sauces

Chunky Italian red sauce (p 157) or
Hot tomato & eggplant sauce (p 161) or
Roasted capsicum sauce (p 158)

Garnishes *(pp 166-9)*

Chilli oil or
Fresh herbs or
Truffle salt

VEAL MARSALA

OVEN BAKE

MAKES 22 MEATBALLS

INSPIRED BY A CLASSIC VEAL MARSALA RECIPE, THIS DELICIOUS COMBINATION OF SWEET MARSALA WINE, EARTHY MUSHROOM AND SAGE IS CARRIED PERFECTLY BY THE DELICATE VEAL. MARSALA WINE CAN BE FOUND AT MOST WINE STORES AND, GENERALLY SPEAKING, POORER QUALITY MARSALA WINE WORKS BEST WITH THIS RECIPE AS IT TENDS TO BE SWEETER.

- 30 G (1 OZ) DRIED PORCINI MUSHROOMS
- WARM WATER, FOR SOAKING
- 50 G (1¾ OZ) BUTTER
- OLIVE OIL
- ½ BROWN ONION, FINELY DICED
- 300 G (10½ OZ) PORTOBELLO MUSHROOMS, COARSELY CHOPPED
- 20 G (¾ OZ/1 SMALL BUNCH) SAGE, COARSELY CHOPPED
- 200 ML (7 FL OZ) MARSALA WINE
- JUICE OF ½ LEMON
- 125 G (4½ OZ) DRY BREADCRUMBS
- 1 KG (2 LB 4 OZ) MINCED (GROUND) VEAL
- 1 EGG

Soak the dried porcini mushrooms in the warm water until they become soft and rehydrated. Strain, then coarsely chop the porcini mushrooms and set aside.

Heat up the butter and olive oil in a frying pan over low heat, add the onion and stir through. Add the portobello mushrooms and half the sage and cook gently for around 2 minutes.

Increase the heat to medium, gradually adding the Marsala wine (about 1 tablespoon at a time), stirring the mixture continuously so that the mushrooms absorb the wine. Once all the wine has been added, introduce the porcini mushrooms and reduce the heat to low. Add the lemon juice and stir through. The mixture should be fairly wet at this stage. Add the breadcrumbs to soak up all the juices and combine thoroughly. Season with salt and pepper and set aside to cool.

Preheat the oven to 160°C (315°F).

In a mixing bowl, season the veal with salt and pepper, add the remainder of the sage and the egg. Add the cooled Marsala mix and combine together using your hands. Roll the mixture into 80 g (2¾ oz) balls.

Spray a baking tray with olive oil and carefully place the meatballs in the tray. Bake the meatballs in a dry oven for 14 minutes.

Serve immediately.

Sotto palle

Creamy polenta (p 144) or
Grilled mushrooms with taleggio cheese (p 150) or
Simple mushroom risotto (p 149)

Sauces

Butter & sage sauce (p 159) or
Gorgonzola cheese sauce (p 156) or
White sauce (p 158)

Garnishes *(pp 166-9)*

Hazelnut pangrattato or
Micro herbs or
Parmesan crisps

VENISON & VEAL

OVEN BAKE

MAKES 22 MEATBALLS

VENISON IS A RICH AND DEEPLY FLAVOURED GAME MEAT, WHICH IS LEAN AND HAS VERY LITTLE FAT CONTENT. THIS RECIPE COMBINES VENISON WITH VEAL TO STRIKE A NICE BALANCE OF FLAVOUR AND TEXTURE. GENERALLY A FARMED PRODUCT, VENISON CAN BE PROCURED FROM YOUR LOCAL BUTCHER.

- 40 G (1½ OZ) BUTTER
- ½ SMALL BROWN ONION, DICED
- 750 G (1 LB 10 OZ) MINCED (GROUND) VENISON
- 250 G (9 OZ) MINCED (GROUND) VEAL
- 55 G (2 OZ/½ CUP) DRY BREADCRUMBS
- 25 G (1 OZ/¼ CUP) FINELY GRATED PARMESAN CHEESE
- 2 TEASPOONS DRIED OREGANO
- 30 G (1 OZ/1 SMALL BUNCH) FLAT-LEAF (ITALIAN) PARSLEY, LEAVES PICKED AND CHOPPED
- 2 GARLIC CLOVES, FINELY DICED
- 1 EGG
- ZEST OF 1 ORANGE
- OLIVE OIL SPRAY, FOR BAKING

Preheat the oven to 160°C (315°F) and add a small ovenproof saucer of water to the back of the oven to create humidity.

Heat up the butter in a frying pan over medium heat, add the onion and cook for about 3–4 minutes. Set aside to cool.

Combine the cooled onion and all the remaining ingredients in a mixing bowl, gently mixing everything together with your hands. Roll the mixture into 60 g (2¼ oz) balls.

Spray a baking tray with olive oil and carefully place the meatballs in the tray. Bake them in the humid oven for 14 minutes.

Serve immediately.

Sotto palle

Creamy polenta (p 144) or
Lasagne sheets (p 146) or
Simple mushroom risotto (p 149)

Sauces

Creamy mushroom sauce (p 164) or
Horseradish cream (p 162) or
Red wine & beef stock sauce (p 163)

Garnishes *(pp 166-9)*

Citrus zest or
Grated cheese or
Pickled zucchini

BEEF WITH GREEN SAUCE

OVEN BAKE
SHALLOW-FRY

MAKES *26* MEATBALLS

YOUR FAVOURITE SAUCE OR CONDIMENT CAN OFTEN BE COMBINED WITH MINCED (GROUND) MEAT TO CREATE A DELICIOUS MEATBALL. HERE WE'VE MATCHED GREEN SAUCE WITH BEEF AND VEAL. THE BEEF GIVES THE MEATBALLS DEPTH OF FLAVOUR AND THE VEAL CARRIES THE SAUCE AND ADDS A DELICATE TEXTURE.

- 500 G (1 LB 2 OZ) MINCED (GROUND) BEEF
- 500 G (1 LB 2 OZ) MINCED (GROUND) VEAL
- 250 G (9 OZ) FRESH RICOTTA CHEESE
- 2 EGGS, WHISKED
- 160 ML (5¼ FL OZ) GREEN SAUCE (P 164), PLUS EXTRA (OPTIONAL)
- 40 G (1½ OZ/⅓ CUP) DRY BREADCRUMBS, PLUS EXTRA IF NEEDED
- OLIVE OIL SPRAY, FOR BAKING
- VEGETABLE OIL, FOR FRYING

Preheat the oven to 160°C (315°F) and add a small ovenproof saucer of water to the back of the oven to create humidity.

In a mixing bowl, season the meats with salt and pepper. Add the ricotta cheese, eggs and the Green Sauce to your liking (see note below). Add the breadcrumbs, adjusting the amount accordingly. Roll the mixture into 60 g (2¼ oz) balls with your hands.

Spray a baking tray with olive oil and carefully place the meatballs in the tray. Bake in the humid oven for 14–16 minutes.

Pour vegetable oil into the frying pan until it's 1–3 cm (½–1¼ in) deep and place over medium heat until the oil is hot. Finish the cooking by shallow-frying the balls for 2–3 minutes on each side until they form a nice brown crust.

Serve immediately.

Note: Adjust the amount of Green Sauce to your liking. If using more sauce, add more breadcrumbs to ensure the mixture isn't too moist.

Sotto palle

Basic peperonata (p 151) or
Buttered risoni & peas (p 144) or
Fried pickled zucchini (p 148)

Sauces

Butter & sage sauce (p 159) or
Chunky Italian red sauce (p 157) or
Green sauce (p 164)

Garnishes *(pp 166-9)*

Fresh herbs or
Fried sage or
Herb oil

VEAL, PORK & LAMB WITH CARAMELISED ONION & LEEK

MAKES 25 MEATBALLS

THESE TASTY MEATBALLS ARE SURPRISINGLY RICH AND HAVE A WONDERFUL SWEETNESS GENERATED BY THE CARAMELISED ONIONS. THE INTRODUCTION OF WHITE WINE AND CREAM CHEESE MAKES THESE MEATBALLS SUPER TENDER AND DELECTABLE.

- 1 LARGE BROWN ONION, DICED
- 75 G (2½ OZ) BUTTER
- 3 TABLESPOONS OLIVE OIL
- 2 GARLIC CLOVES, FINELY DICED
- 120 G (4¼ OZ) LEEK, PALE PART ONLY, FINELY DICED
- 50 G (1¾ OZ/1 LARGE BUNCH) FLAT-LEAF (ITALIAN) PARSLEY, LEAVES PICKED AND FINELY CHOPPED
- 6 TARRAGON STALKS, CHOPPED
- 10 SAGE LEAVES, FINELY CHOPPED
- 2 ANCHOVY FILLETS, FINELY CHOPPED
- ZEST OF ½ ORANGE
- 75 ML (2¼ FL OZ) WHITE WINE
- 3 TABLESPOONS CREAM CHEESE
- 55 G (2 OZ/½ CUP) DRY BREADCRUMBS
- 300 G (10½ OZ) MINCED (GROUND) VEAL
- 300 G (10½ OZ) MINCED (GROUND) PORK
- 150 G (5½ OZ) MINCED (GROUND) LAMB
- 1 EGG
- OLIVE OIL SPRAY, FOR BAKING
- VEGETABLE OIL, FOR FRYING

In a heavy-based saucepan with a lid, caramelise the onion with a pinch of salt over low heat until it's deep brown in colour. This will take around 20 minutes. Make sure you stir the onions occasionally to avoid them sticking to the base of the pan.

Once browned, add the butter and the olive oil and then the garlic, leek, parsley, tarragon, sage, anchovy fillets and orange zest, and cook gently for 3–5 minutes. Add the white wine and cream cheese and cook for about 4–6 minutes until the liquid reduces by half. Add the breadcrumbs to the pan to soak up the rest of the cooking juices. Set this mixture aside to cool.

Preheat the oven to 200°C (400°F).

In a mixing bowl, add the meats and season with salt and pepper. Add the egg and the cooled mixture and combine. Roll the mixture into 50 g (1¾ oz) balls.

Spray a baking tray with olive oil and carefully place the meatballs in the tray. Bake the meatballs in a dry oven for 10 minutes.

Pour some vegetable oil into a deep frying pan until it's approximately 1–3 cm (½–1¼ in) deep, and place over medium–high heat. Finish the meatballs by shallow-frying for 2 minutes until golden.

Serve immediately.

Sotto palle

Buttered risoni & peas (p 144) or
Couscous with muscatels & pistachios (p 148) or
Roasted fennel with almond & lemon butter crumb (p 153)

Sauces

Chunky Italian red sauce (p 157) or
Italian veal jus (p 156) or
White sauce (p 158)

Garnishes (pp 166-9)

Grated cheese or
Hazelnut pangrattato or
Micro herbs

SPICED LAMB

OVEN BAKE

MAKES *18* MEATBALLS

LAMB HAS A DISTINCT FLAVOUR AND TEXTURE THAT GOES PERFECTLY WITH THE MIDDLE EASTERN SPICES USED IN THIS RECIPE. YOU CAN MAKE THE SPICE MIXTURE YOURSELF, OR PURCHASE A SPICE MIX OF YOUR CHOICE TO CREATE YOUR OWN VERSION OF THIS RECIPE.

- 150 G (5½ OZ) CHUNKY ITALIAN RED SAUCE (P 157)
- 1 KG (2 LB 4 OZ) MINCED (GROUND) LAMB
- 1 EGG
- 30 G (1 OZ/¼ CUP) DRY BREADCRUMBS
- 35 G (1¼ OZ/⅓ CUP) FINELY GRATED PARMESAN CHEESE
- 4 THYME SPRIGS, FINELY CHOPPED
- 30 G (1 OZ/1 SMALL BUNCH) FLAT-LEAF (ITALIAN) PARSLEY, LEAVES PICKED AND FINELY CHOPPED
- OLIVE OIL SPRAY, FOR BAKING

SPICE MIX

- 1 TABLESPOON CORIANDER SEEDS
- 1 TABLESPOON CUMIN SEEDS
- 2 TEASPOONS GARLIC POWDER
- 1 TEASPOON ONION POWDER
- 1 TABLESPOON DRIED OREGANO
- 1 TEASPOON MILD PAPRIKA
- 1 PINCH CINNAMON POWDER
- 1 TEASPOON CHILLI FLAKES
- 1 PINCH CURRY POWDER

Preheat the oven to 160°C (315°F) and add a small ovenproof saucer of water to the back of the oven to create humidity.

To make the spice mix, toast the coriander seeds and cumin seeds in a dry frying pan over low heat until they start to release their aromas. Once toasted, combine with the rest of the spices in a small bowl and mix together well.

Add 2 tablespoons of the spice mix directly to the Red Sauce at this stage to ensure the spices are later distributed evenly throughout the lamb.

In a mixing bowl, combine the lamb, egg, breadcrumbs, parmesan cheese, thyme, parsley and spiced Red Sauce, and season with salt and pepper. Gently fold the minced lamb with your hands until all of the ingredients are evenly combined. Using your hands, roll the mixture into 70 g (2½ oz) balls.

Spray a baking tray with olive oil and carefully place the meatballs in the tray. Bake the balls in the humid oven for 18 minutes.

Serve immediately.

Sotto palle

Buttered risoni & peas (p 144) or
Fregola, fresh ricotta & pepitas (p 145) or
Roasted pumpkin (p 152)

Sauces

Green sauce (p 164) or
Hot tomato & eggplant sauce (p 161) or
Labna (p 157)

Garnishes *(pp 166-9)*

Chilli oil or
Micro herbs or
Toasted pistachios

LAMB & PAPRIKA

OVEN BAKE
SHALLOW-FRY

MAKES 22 MEATBALLS

SWEET LAMB AND FIERY PAPRIKA – WHAT A MATCH! THESE FLAVOUR-PACKED MEATBALLS ARE AMAZINGLY SOFT AND DELICATE, THANKS TO THE ADDITION OF PORK FAT. ASK YOUR BUTCHER FOR SOME FIRM WHITE MINCED (GROUND) PORK FAT FROM AROUND THE BELLY.

- 100 ML (3½ FL OZ) EXTRA VIRGIN OLIVE OIL
- 1 LARGE RED ONION, DICED
- 1 TEASPOON (IN TOTAL) FRESHLY GROUND CORIANDER, CUMIN AND FENNEL SEEDS
- 100 G (3½ OZ) FRESH RICOTTA CHEESE
- 1 KG (2 LB 4 OZ) MINCED (GROUND) LAMB
- 150 G (5½ OZ) MINCED (GROUND) PORK FAT
- 2 EGGS, BEATEN
- ¼ TEASPOON GARLIC POWDER
- ¼ TEASPOON SMOKED PAPRIKA
- 40 G (1½ OZ/⅓ CUP) FINE DRY BREADCRUMBS
- 20 G (¾ OZ/1 SMALL BUNCH) THYME, LEAVES PICKED
- 30 G (1 OZ/1 SMALL BUNCH FLAT-LEAF (ITALIAN) PARSLEY, LEAVES PICKED AND CHOPPED
- SALT FLAKES
- OLIVE OIL SPRAY, FOR BAKING
- VEGETABLE OIL, FOR FRYING

Set a frying pan over medium heat and add a generous amount of the olive oil (around one-third of a cup). Add the onion and cook until softened (about 4–6 minutes). Stir in the ground spices and remove from the heat.

Place the onion mix in a mixing bowl and allow to cool to room temperature. Add the ricotta cheese, meats, egg, spices, breadcrumbs and herbs. Finish with a good splash of olive oil (about 1 tablespoon), season with salt flakes and freshly ground black pepper, and gently combine. Chill in the refrigerator for at least 45 minutes.

Preheat the oven to 160°C (315°F).

Remove the mixture from the refrigerator and gently roll 60 g (2¼ oz) meatballs with your hands.

Spray a baking tray with olive oil, carefully place the meatballs in the tray and bake in a dry oven for 12 minutes.

Pour vegetable oil into the frying pan until it's 1–3 cm (½–1¼ in) deep, and place over medium heat until the oil is hot. Test the oil temperature by dropping in a pinch of plain flour. If it sizzles away almost immediately without burning, the oil is at the right temperature. Finish the cooking by shallow-frying the balls for 2–3 minutes on each side until they form a nice brown crust.

Serve while hot.

Sotto palle

Buttered risoni & peas (p 144) or
Fregola, fresh ricotta & pepitas (p 145) or
Toasted quinoa, lentils & corn (p 152)

Sauces

Hot tomato & eggplant sauce (p 161) or
Roasted capsicum sauce (p 158) or
White sauce (p 158)

Garnishes *(pp 166-9)*

Pickled zucchini or
Salt flakes or
Toasted pistachios

LAMB, ROASTED POTATO & ROSEMARY

OVEN BAKE

MAKES *18* MEATBALLS

LIKE A SUNDAY ROAST, THESE MEATBALLS COMBINE SOME CLASSIC INGREDIENTS TO CREATE A WONDERFULLY NOSTALGIC MEATBALL EXPERIENCE. THE SCENT OF ROASTING POTATOES AND ROSEMARY ARE SURE TO LEAVE YOU AND YOUR GUESTS SALIVATING IN ANTICIPATION OF A GREAT MEAL.

250 G (9 OZ) ROASTING POTATOES, CUT INTO SMALL CHUNKS
4 GARLIC CLOVES
1 TABLESPOON CHOPPED ROSEMARY
1 ONION, SLICED
OLIVE OIL
1 TABLESPOON JUNIPER BERRIES
1 TABLESPOON CORIANDER SEEDS
750 G (1 LB 10 OZ) MINCED (GROUND) LAMB
25 G (1 OZ/¼ CUP) FINELY GRATED PARMESAN CHEESE
2½ TABLESPOONS DRY BREADCRUMBS
1 EGG
OLIVE OIL SPRAY, FOR BAKING

Preheat the oven to 160°C (315°F).

In a roasting tray, place the potatoes, garlic, rosemary and onion, and drizzle with olive oil. Bake until the potatoes are cooked (about 1½ hours).

Remove the tray from the oven, place the potatoes in a large bowl and mash the mix with a fork before setting aside to cool.

Toast the juniper berries and coriander seeds in a dry frying pan over medium heat until they begin to give off a lovely aroma (but before they take on any colour). This will take approximately 3–5 minutes. Remove them from the pan and grind them down in a mortar and pestle.

Season the minced lamb with salt and pepper in a large mixing bowl. Add the cooled potatoes, ground juniper and coriander, parmesan cheese, breadcrumbs and egg, and combine.

Add a small ovenproof saucer of water to the back of the oven to create humidity.

Using your hands, gently roll the mixture into 60 g (2¼ oz) balls.

Spray a baking tray with olive oil and carefully place the meatballs in the tray. Bake in the humid oven for 12 minutes.

Serve immediately.

Sotto palle

Couscous with muscatels & pistachios (p 148) or
Roasted pumpkin (p 152) or
Super potato smash (p 145)

Sauces

Chunky Italian red sauce (p 157) or
Hot tomato & eggplant sauce (p 161) or
Red wine & beef stock sauce (p 163)

Garnishes *(pp 166-9)*

Fresh herbs or
Hazelnut pangrattato or
Salt flakes

MINI MEATBALLS

PAN-FRY

MAKES *30* MEATBALLS

MINI MEATBALLS MAKE THE PERFECT STARTER OR CANAPÉ AND CAN BE HIGHLY VERSATILE FOR USE IN SOUPS AND WITH PASTA. UTILISE ANY OF THE MEATBALL RECIPES FOUND IN THIS BOOK, ROLL SMALLER 20 G (3/4 OZ) BALLS AND SIMPLY PAN-FRY THEM SO THEY BROWN ON ALL SIDES.

- 500 G (1 LB 2 OZ) MINCED (GROUND) BEEF
- 1 TEASPOON PAPRIKA
- 25 G (1 OZ/¼ CUP) FINELY GRATED PARMESAN CHEESE
- 2 EGGS
- 15 G (½ OZ/½ SMALL BUNCH) FLAT-LEAF (ITALIAN) PARSLEY, LEAVES PICKED AND FINELY CHOPPED
- 2 TEASPOONS DRIED OREGANO
- 1 GARLIC CLOVE, CRUSHED
- 2 TABLESPOONS DRY BREADCRUMBS
- VEGETABLE OIL, FOR FRYING

In a large mixing bowl, season the beef with salt and pepper. Add the remaining ingredients and work the mixture well for around 2 minutes, until it starts to become sticky. Roll the mixture into 20 g (3/4 oz) balls and set them aside in the refrigerator to cool for 30 minutes.

Heat up some vegetable oil in a frying pan over medium heat. Once the oil is hot, introduce the mini balls a few at a time, taking care not to overcrowd the pan. You can do this in stages. Constantly move the pan in a circling motion. This will help the balls roll around the pan and cook evenly. Do this until the balls form a nice brown crust on all sides. This should take around 3–4 minutes.

Once cooked, place the mini balls in a bowl and serve with dipping sauces and garnishes.

Note: If planning on using a toothpick to serve, mini balls might require extra firmness so they can be lifted with a toothpick. To achieve this, work the meat a little more than you normally would and add a quarter more egg than prescribed in the recipe – this will bind the ball a little more and help it stick to the toothpick or mini fork.

Sauces

Barbecue sauce (p 161) or
Green sauce (p 164) or
Labna (p 157)

Garnishes (pp 166-9)

Chilli oil or
Citrus zest or
Micro herbs

BREAKFAST MEATBALLS

MAKES *33* MEATBALLS

ALL YOUR FAVOURITE BREAKFAST ITEMS COMBINE IN THIS MEATBALL TO CREATE ONE TASTY DELIGHT. FEEL FREE TO ADD ANY OTHER BREAKFAST TREATS TO TAILOR-MAKE YOUR OWN VERSION OF THIS MEATBALL.

220 G (7¾ OZ/1½ CUPS) BABY (OR CHERRY) TOMATOES
300 G (10½ OZ) BACON, DICED
1 SMALL ONION, DICED
250 G (9 OZ) PORTOBELLO MUSHROOMS, DICED
1 KG (2 LB 4 OZ) MINCED (GROUND) PORK
2 TABLESPOONS TOMATO SAUCE (KETCHUP)
4 EGG YOLKS
6 ROSEMARY SPRIGS, LEAVES PICKED AND CHOPPED
15 G (½ OZ/½ SMALL BUNCH) FLAT-LEAF (ITALIAN) PARSLEY, LEAVES PICKED AND CHOPPED
40 G (1½ OZ/⅓ CUP) DRY BREADCRUMBS
OLIVE OIL

Preheat the oven to 200°C (400°F).

Roast the tomatoes in the oven for around 15–20 minutes, or until the skin scorches and the tomatoes start to break down. Set aside to cool.

Cook off the bacon in a frying pan over high heat for about 3–4 minutes. Before they start to brown, add the onions. Cook for around 3 minutes, then add the mushrooms and cook until everything becomes nice and brown. Remove the bacon, onion and mushroom mixture from the pan and set aside to cool.

Slice the cooled roasted tomatoes in half.

In a mixing bowl, season the pork with salt and pepper. Add the tomato sauce, egg yolks, rosemary, parsley, breadcrumbs and the cooled cooked items (roasted tomatoes, onion, mushroom and bacon). Mix everything together with your hands and roll the mixture into 50 g (1¾ oz) balls.

Turn the oven down to 180°C (350°F).

Heat up a good drizzle of olive oil in an ovenproof frying pan over medium–high heat. Once the oil is hot, add the meatballs, taking care not to overcrowd the pan. You can do this in stages. Constantly move the pan in a circling motion. This will help the balls roll around and brown evenly. This should take around 5 minutes.

Transfer the pan to the dry oven for around 8 minutes.

Serve hot.

Sotto palle

Basic peperonata (p 151) or
Cheesy bread (p 153) or
Italian beans (p 154)

Sauces

Aioli (p 160) or
Barbecue sauce (p 161) or
Napoli cruda (p 165)

Garnishes *(pp 166-9)*

Chilli oil or
Herb oil or
Salt flakes

LE CREUSET

BEEF, PORK & PROSCIUTTO

MAKES 22 MEATBALLS

Here's a classic Italian recipe, which combines a duet of meats with prosciutto. Oregano and fennel complement the beef and pork while the prosciutto creates depth with its rich, salty flavour.

150 G (5½ OZ) DAY-OLD BREAD SLICES
60 ML (2 FL OZ/¼ CUP) MILK
300 G (10½ OZ) MINCED (GROUND) PORK
300 G (10½ OZ) MINCED (GROUND) BEEF
SALT FLAKES
60 G (2¼ OZ) PROSCIUTTO, FINELY CHOPPED
60 G (2¼ OZ) MINCED (GROUND) PORK FAT
30 G (1 OZ/1 SMALL BUNCH) FLAT-LEAF (ITALIAN) PARSLEY, LEAVES PICKED AND CHOPPED
1 TEASPOON OREGANO
1 TEASPOON FENNEL SEEDS
1 TEASPOON CHILLI FLAKES
115 G (4 OZ/½ CUP) FRESH RICOTTA CHEESE
2 EGGS
OLIVE OIL SPRAY, FOR BAKING
OLIVE OIL (OPTIONAL)
1.5 KG (3 LB 5 OZ) CHUNKY ITALIAN RED SAUCE (P 157) (OPTIONAL)

Preheat the oven to 180°C (350°F).

Soak the bread in the milk for several minutes, then squeeze out the excess milk and tear up the bread into small pieces.

In a mixing bowl, season the pork and beef generously with salt flakes and pepper. Add the bread, prosciutto, pork fat, parsley, oregano, fennel seeds, chilli flakes, ricotta cheese and eggs, and gently combine. Roll the mixture into 50 g (1¾ oz) balls.

Spray a baking tray with olive oil and carefully place the balls in the tray.

Bake in the dry oven for 8 minutes.

If you are frying the meatballs, heat up a drizzle of olive oil in a frying pan over medium heat. Once the oil is hot, introduce the meatballs a few at a time, taking care not to overcrowd the pan. You can do this in stages. Constantly move the pan in a circling motion. This will help the balls roll around the pan and achieve a nice even brown colour. This should take around 4 minutes.

If you are poaching the meatballs, pour the Red Sauce into a large saucepan and set on the stovetop over low heat. Transfer the meatballs from oven to saucepan and gently simmer for 15 minutes until cooked all the way through.

Serve over your sotto palle immediately.

Sotto palle

Creamy polenta *(p 144)* *or*
Minestrone *(p 154)* *or*
Super potato smash *(p 145)*

Sauces

Chunky Italian red sauce *(p 157)* *or*
Italian veal jus *(p 156)* *or*
Red wine & beef stock sauce *(p 163)*

Garnishes (pp 166-9)

Fresh red chilli or
Prosciutto crisps or
Truffle salt

VEAL & PORK WITH POLENTA & MUSHROOM

MAKES 20 MEATBALLS

THANKS TO THE CHUNKS OF POLENTA, THESE DELICIOUS BALLS MAKE A HEARTY MEAL, EVEN ON THEIR OWN. PANCETTA, MUSHROOM AND A HINT OF TRUFFLE SALT ROUND OUT THESE MEATBALLS AND MAKE THEM A CERTAIN HIT.

65 G (2¼ OZ) POLENTA (CORNMEAL), PLUS EXTRA FOR COATING
100 G (3½ OZ) PANCETTA PIECES
200 G (7 OZ) PORTOBELLO MUSHROOMS, DICED
70 G (2½ OZ) BUTTER
2 GARLIC CLOVES, FINELY DICED
½ FRESH RED CHILLI, FINELY CHOPPED
OLIVE OIL
200 G (7 OZ) MINCED (GROUND) PORK
200 G (7 OZ) MINCED (GROUND) VEAL
2 TEASPOONS FRESHLY GRATED NUTMEG
PINCH OF TRUFFLE SALT
ZEST OF ½ ORANGE
25 G (1 OZ/¼ CUP) FINELY GRATED PARMESAN CHEESE
10 SAGE LEAVES, CHOPPED
OLIVE OIL SPRAY, FOR BAKING

Cook the polenta according to the packet instructions and set aside to cool until it becomes firm.

Add the pancetta to a dry frying pan and cook for several minutes over medium heat, then add the mushrooms, butter, garlic and chilli and a small drizzle of olive oil. Cook until the mushrooms take on a nice deep-brown colour and are soft to touch. This will take around 8 minutes. Set the mixture aside to cool.

Preheat the oven to 160°C (315°F) and add a small ovenproof saucer of water to the back of the oven to create humidity.

Break up the cooked polenta into small chunks.

Season the pork and veal in a mixing bowl and add the rest of the ingredients, including the polenta and the cooled pancetta mushroom mix. Combine thoroughly and form 50 g (1¾ oz) balls, then roll the balls in the extra (uncooked) polenta.

Carefully place the balls in a baking tray and gently spray them with olive oil spray. Bake in the humid oven for around 8 minutes.

Serve while hot.

Sotto palle

Creamy polenta (p 144) or
Basic peperonata (p 151) or
Simple mushroom risotto (p 149)

Sauces

Creamy mushroom sauce (p 164) or
Italian veal jus (p 156) or
Slow-cooked meat sauce (p 160)

Garnishes (pp 166-9)

Chilli oil or
Flavoured butter or
Fresh herbs

PORK, BEEF & GINGER

MAKES *18* MEATBALLS

Inspired by Japanese cuisine, these pork, beef and ginger balls are incredibly fragrant and very easy to make. The use of ginger and bamboo shoots lightens the dish and the addition of soy sauce and mirin gives it that quintessential Japanese flavour.

- 400 G (14 OZ) MINCED (GROUND) PORK
- 400 G (14 OZ) MINCED (GROUND) BEEF
- 2 SPRING ONIONS (SCALLIONS), THINLY SLICED
- 60 G (2¼ OZ/1 CUP) PANKO (JAPANESE-STYLE) BREADCRUMBS
- 50 G (1¾ OZ/⅓ CUP) FINELY DICED BAMBOO SHOOTS
- 2 GARLIC CLOVES, FINELY DICED
- 2½ TEASPOONS GRATED FRESH GINGER
- 1 EGG, LIGHTLY BEATEN
- 2 TABLESPOONS SOY SAUCE
- 1 TABLESPOON MIRIN (RICE WINE)
- VEGETABLE OIL, FOR FRYING
- OLIVE OIL SPRAY, FOR BAKING

Combine all of the ingredients together in a mixing bowl and use your hands to roll the mixture into 60 g (2¼ oz) balls. Set these aside in the refrigerator for 2 hours to allow the flavours to develop.

Preheat the oven to 160°C (315°F).

Heat up some vegetable oil in a large frying pan over medium heat. Once the oil is hot, introduce the meatballs a few at a time, taking care not to overcrowd the pan. You can do this in stages. Constantly move the pan in a circling motion. This will help the balls roll around the pan and achieve a nice even colour. This should take around 2 minutes.

Spray a baking tray with olive oil and carefully place the balls in the tray.

Cook them in the dry oven for 10–12 minutes and serve immediately.

Sotto palle

Buttered edamame (p 147) or
Fried pickled zucchini (p 148) or
Wasabi slaw (p 151)

Sauces

Aioli (p 160) or
Barbecue sauce (p 161) or
Spicy hoisin sauce with ginger & garlic (p 163)

Garnishes *(pp 166-9)*

Fresh herbs or
Fresh red chilli or
Herb oil

PORK, PEANUT & WATER CHESTNUT

MAKES *30* MEATBALLS

USING SIMILAR INGREDIENTS TO A TRADITIONAL SAN CHOY BAU, THIS INCREDIBLY TASTY MEATBALL IS A PERFECT EXAMPLE OF HOW TO TURN A TIMELESS CLASSIC INTO A SPHERICAL DELIGHT. ONCE COOKED, SIMPLY PLACE EACH BALL IN A LETTUCE LEAF AND SERVE.

1 KG (2 LB 4 OZ) MINCED (GROUND) PORK
4 GARLIC CLOVES, CRUSHED
60 G (2¼ OZ) GINGER, GRATED, PLUS EXTRA TO SERVE
120 G (4¼ OZ) WATER CHESTNUTS, DICED
2 TABLESPOONS OYSTER SAUCE
2 TABLESPOONS HOISIN SAUCE
100 ML (3½ FL OZ) SOY SAUCE
2 TABLESPOONS JAPANESE MAYONNAISE
1 WHITE ONION, FINELY DICED
ZEST OF 1 SMALL LIME
50 G (1¾ OZ/1 LARGE BUNCH) CORIANDER (CILANTRO), LEAVES PICKED AND CHOPPED
1 EGG, WHISKED
120 G (4¼ OZ) ROASTED PEANUTS, COOLED AND CRUSHED
SESAME OIL
BEAN SPROUTS (OPTIONAL)
2 FRESH GREEN CHILLIES, SLICED (OPTIONAL)
JUICE OF 1 LIME, FOR DRIZZLING (OPTIONAL)

In a mixing bowl, combine all the ingredients (except the peanuts and sesame oil) and season with a pinch of white pepper and salt. Set the mixture aside to cool in the refrigerator for up to 1 hour. This will allow the aromatics to infuse into the pork.

Remove the mixture from the refrigerator, add the peanuts and combine. Using your hands, roll the mixture into 50 g (1¾ oz) balls.

Preheat the oven to 180°C (350°F) and add a small ovenproof saucer of water to the back of the oven to create humidity.

Heat a drizzle of sesame oil in an ovenproof frying pan over medium heat. Introduce the meatballs a few at a time into the hot pan, taking care not to overcrowd the pan. Constantly move the pain in a circling motion. This will help the balls roll around the pan and achieve a nice even brown colour. You can do this in stages. This should take around 3–5 minutes.

Once each ball has colour, add them all to the pan, transfer to the humid oven and cook for 8 minutes.

Serve immediately on lettuce leaves.

Note: You can buy the peanuts already roasted, but if you want to do them yourself, simply spread them out on a roasting tray and bake them in a dry oven at 160°C (315°F) for around 15 minutes.

Note: For extra crunch and heat, add bean sprouts, some grated ginger and sliced green chilli to the lettuce leaves with the meatballs. Drizzle with lime juice.

Sotto palle

Buttered edamame (p 147) or
Toasted quinoa, lentils & corn (p 152) or
Wasabi slaw (p 151)

Sauces

Aioli (p 160) or
Horseradish cream (p 162) or
Spicy hoisin sauce with ginger & garlic (p 163)

Garnishes *(pp 166-9)*

Citrus zest or
Edible flowers or
Micro herbs

PORK & BEEF WITH EGGPLANT, DATES & BROWN RICE

SHALLOW-FRY

MAKES 28 MEATBALLS

EGGPLANT IS A WONDERFUL INGREDIENT TO USE IN MEATBALLS, AS IT TENDS TO HOLD MOISTURE. HERE IT'S COMBINED WITH BROWN RICE, WHICH MAKES THESE MEATBALLS SUPER SOFT AND TENDER.

150 G (5½ OZ) MEDIUM-GRAIN BROWN RICE
50 G (1¾ OZ/⅓ CUP) PINE NUTS
OLIVE OIL
150 G (5½ OZ) EGGPLANT (AUBERGINE), FINELY DICED
12 SAGE LEAVES, CHOPPED
2 GARLIC CLOVES, FINELY DICED
3 TEASPOONS TOMATO PASTE (CONCENTRATED PURÉE)
1 SMALL ONION, DICED
3 DATES, PITTED AND CHOPPED
600 G (1 LB 5 OZ) MINCED (GROUND) PORK
150 G (5½ OZ) MINCED (GROUND) BEEF
1½ EGGS, WHISKED
PLAIN (ALL-PURPOSE) FLOUR, FOR COATING
VEGETABLE OIL, FOR FRYING

Cook the brown rice in boiling water until slightly overcooked, then set it aside. This should take no longer than 45 minutes.

Toast the pine nuts in a dry frying pan over medium heat for a few minutes until browned on all sides.

Heat a drizzle of olive oil in a frying pan over medium heat and sauté the eggplant for about 5 minutes. Add the sage, toasted pine nuts, garlic, tomato paste and half of the onion, and cook for another 5 minutes. Add the rice and dates to the pan and combine. Set this mixture aside in the refrigerator to cool.

In a large mixing bowl, season the meat with salt and pepper. Add the rest of the onion, the eggplant mixture and the whisked egg, and combine thoroughly. Using your hands, roll the mixture into 50 g (1¾ oz) balls and toss them through the flour.

Pour some vegetable oil into a deep frying pan until it's approximately 1–3 cm (½–1¼ in) deep, and place over medium–high heat. Introduce the meatballs a few at a time. They should start to sizzle on contact. Cook the meatballs on one side for around 3 minutes before rolling them over to the other side to cook for another 3 minutes. This will form a nice brown crust around the entire meatball.

Serve while hot.

Sotto palle

Basic peperonata (p 151) or
Creamy polenta, grilled (p 144) or
Roasted fennel with almond & lemon butter crumb (p 153)

Sauces

Butter & sage sauce (p 159) or
Chunky Italian red sauce (p 157) or
Slow-cooked meat sauce (p 160)

Garnishes *(pp 166-9)*

Citrus zest or
Grated cheese or
Hazelnut pangrattato

BIG BALLS

OVEN BAKE

MAKES 6 MEATBALLS

Two meatballs feature in Big Balls, with one nestled inside another. Apply this method to any of your favourite meatball combinations to come up with interesting flavour profiles. The idea is to create a soft and juicy centre meatball, enveloped in a more robust outer meatball.

INNER BALLS

- 30 G (1 OZ) BUTTER
- OLIVE OIL
- 1 SMALL LEEK, PALE PART ONLY, FINELY CHOPPED
- 30 G (1 OZ) BACON, FINELY DICED
- 150 G (5½ OZ) MINCED (GROUND) PORK
- 25 G (1 OZ/¼ CUP) FINELY GRATED PARMESAN CHEESE

OUTER BALLS

- 500 G (1 LB 2 OZ) MINCED (GROUND) BEEF
- 2 GARLIC CLOVES, FINELY DICED
- ½ WHITE ONION, FINELY DICED
- 2 TABLESPOONS CHUNKY ITALIAN RED SAUCE (P 157)
- ½ TEASPOON CHILLI FLAKES
- 20 G (¾ OZ) DRY BREADCRUMBS
- 30 G (1 OZ/1 SMALL BUNCH) FLAT-LEAF (ITALIAN) PARSLEY, LEAVES PICKED, FINELY CHOPPED
- 1 TEASPOON DRIED OREGANO
- 25 G (1 OZ/¼ CUP) FINELY GRATED PARMESAN CHEESE
- 2 EGGS
- OLIVE OIL SPRAY, FOR BAKING

To make the inner balls, heat up the butter and a drizzle of olive oil in a frying pan over medium heat, add the leek and cook for about 3–4 minutes until softened. Add the bacon and cook for a further 5 minutes. Set the mixture aside to cool.

In a mixing bowl, season the pork with salt and pepper, then add the cooled leek and bacon mixture. Using your hands, roll the mixture into 40 g (1½ oz) balls, cover them in parmesan cheese and place them on a tray. Set them aside in the refrigerator.

Preheat the oven to 180°C (350°F) and add a small ovenproof saucer of water to the back of the oven to create humidity.

To make the outer balls, combine all the ingredients together in a mixing bowl and form two 80 g (2¾ oz) patties. Take the pre-made pork ball and place it in the centre of one patty in the cup of your hand. Place the other pattie on top and, using cupped hands, form one large ball. Continue to make big balls with the remaining beef mixture and the pork balls.

Spray a large indented bakers tray with olive oil and carefully place the balls in the tray. Cook in the humid oven for 20 minutes. Remove one of the big balls and slice it in half to ensure the entire ball is cooked all the way through.

Serve while hot.

Sotto palle

Creamy polenta (p 144) or
Lasagne sheets (p 146) or
Super potato smash (p 145)

Sauces

Chunky Italian red sauce 📷 (p 157) or
Creamy mushroom sauce (p 164) or
Gorgonzola cheese sauce (p 156)

Garnishes *(pp 166-9)*

Fresh red chilli or
Grated cheese 📷 or
Truffle salt

deBUYER
FRANCE

BACON & BOURBON

OVEN BAKE

MAKES **28** MEATBALLS

A MUST FOR LOVERS OF PORKY GOODNESS, THESE TASTY BACON AND BOURBON BALLS HAVE A SURPRISINGLY SOFT AND DELICATE TEXTURE. FEEL FREE TO USE PANCETTA INSTEAD OF BACON AND ADJUST THE AMOUNT OF CAYENNE PEPPER TO SUIT YOUR TASTE.

- 2 RED CAPSICUMS (PEPPERS)
- 200 G (7 OZ) BACON, DICED
- OLIVE OIL
- 200 ML (7 FL OZ) BOURBON
- 1 KG (2 LB 4 OZ) MINCED (GROUND) PORK
- 2 TABLESPOONS BARBECUE SAUCE (P 161)
- ½ TABLESPOON TABASCO SAUCE
- ½ TEASPOON CAYENNE PEPPER
- 80 G (2¾ OZ/⅔ CUP) DRY BREADCRUMBS
- 3 EGGS
- OLIVE OIL SPRAY, FOR BAKING

Scorch and cook the capsicums by placing them over an open flame or in a hot 200°C (400°F) oven until the skins are black and the flesh is soft. Seed and chop into small pieces (keep the blackened skin as well).

Crisp up the bacon in a frying pan over medium heat with a drizzle of olive oil and a pinch of salt. Once cooked, add the capsicum pieces to the pan.Pour in the bourbon and bring to the boil, stirring for about 2–3 minutes to deglaze the pan. Remove the pan from the heat before all the liquid evaporates and set aside to cool.

In a mixing bowl, season the minced pork with salt and pepper, then add all the remaining ingredients and combine. Place the mixture into the refrigerator to cool for at least 1 hour.

Preheat the oven to 180°C (350°F).

Remove the mixture from the refrigerator and gently roll 60 g (2¼ oz) balls with your hands. The mixture should be fairly wet.

Spray a baking tray with olive oil and carefully place the meatballs into the tray. Bake in the dry oven for 12–14 minutes.

Serve while hot.

Sotto palle

Basic peperonata 📷 *(p 151) or*
Buttered risoni & peas (p 144) or
Roasted pumpkin (p 152)

Sauces

Aioli (p 160) or
Barbecue sauce (p 161) or
Horseradish cream (p 162)

Garnishes *(pp 166-9)*

Chilli oil or
Herb oil or
Micro herbs

BOCCONCINI-STUFFED PORK & VEAL

OVEN BAKE

MAKES 12 MEATBALLS

PACKED WITH FLAVOUR, THESE BIG JUICY BALLS ARE SUPER IMPRESSIVE. WHEN YOU CUT INTO THE MEATBALL, THE WARM BOCCONCINI OOZES OUT OF THE BALL AND COMBINES WITH YOUR SOTTO PALLE TO CREATE A COMPLETE, COMFORTING DISH.

50 G (1¾ OZ) BUTTER
1 DRIED BAY LEAF
40 G (1½ OZ) BACON, FINELY DICED
½ BROWN ONION, FINELY DICED
75 G (2½ OZ) PORTOBELLO MUSHROOMS, FINELY DICED
500 G (1 LB 2 OZ) MINCED (GROUND) PORK
500 G (1 LB 2 OZ) MINCED (GROUND) VEAL
30 G (1 OZ/1 SMALL BUNCH) FLAT-LEAF (ITALIAN) PARSLEY, LEAVES PICKED AND CHOPPED
30 G (1 OZ/1 SMALL BUNCH) BASIL, CHOPPED
35 G (1¼ OZ/⅓ CUP) FINELY GRATED PARMESAN CHEESE
80 G (2¾ OZ/⅔ CUP) DRY BREADCRUMBS, PLUS EXTRA FOR COATING
30 G (1 OZ) CHUNKY ITALIAN RED SAUCE (P 157)
2 EGGS
12 MINI BOCCONCINI
OLIVE OIL SPRAY, FOR BAKING

In a shallow frying pan over low heat, gently warm the butter, bay leaf, bacon and onion until the butter begins to bubble. Add the mushrooms and cook until soft (about 5 minutes). Remove the bay leaf and set the mixture aside to cool.

Preheat the oven to 160°C (315°F).

In a mixing bowl, season the meats with salt and pepper and add the cooled onion, bacon and mushroom mixture. Add the parsley, basil, parmesan cheese, breadcrumbs, Red Sauce and eggs, and gently fold the ingredients with your hands before rolling the mixture into 120 g (4¼ oz) balls.

Once all your balls are formed, use your thumb to create a pocket in the meatball and insert a piece of bocconcini. Re-form the ball around the bocconcini and set each ball aside. Roll each of the balls in breadcrumbs, ensuring each ball is completely coated. This will create a nice crust around each ball.

Spray a baking tray with olive oil and carefully place each ball in the tray. Bake the balls in the dry oven for 14–16 minutes.

It's important to serve these balls immediately so the bocconcini cheese remains melted.

Sotto palle

Buttered risoni & peas (p 144) or
Lasagne sheets (p 146) or
Roasted fennel with almond & lemon butter crumb (p 153)

Sauces

Chunky Italian red sauce (p 157) or
Italian veal jus (p 156) or
White sauce (p 158)

Garnishes *(pp 166-9)*

Hazelnut pangrattato or
Toasted pistachios or
Truffle salt

PORK, FENNEL & ORANGE

OVEN BAKE

MAKES *20* MEATBALLS

VENETIAN IN ORIGIN, PORK AND FENNEL IS A CLASSIC COMBINATION, NOT ONLY FOR MEATBALLS, BUT ALSO IN MANY EUROPEAN SAUSAGES AND SALAMI. THE ADDITION OF ORANGE ZEST LIFTS THE EATING EXPERIENCE BY INTRODUCING ACIDITY TO THE MEATBALLS, HELPING TO CUT THROUGH THE RICHNESS OF THE PORK.

60 G (2¼ OZ) BUTTER
1 TABLESPOON OLIVE OIL
½ SMALL ONION, DICED
2 GARLIC CLOVES, DICED
2 TEASPOONS FENNEL SEEDS
1 TEASPOON CHILLI FLAKES
20 SAGE LEAVES, CHOPPED
1 KG (2 LB 4 OZ) MINCED (GROUND) PORK
2 EGGS
85 G (3 OZ/¾ CUP) DRY BREADCRUMBS
ZEST OF 1 ORANGE
50 G (1¾ OZ/½ CUP) FINELY GRATED PARMESAN CHEESE
OLIVE OIL SPRAY, FOR BAKING

Warm the butter and olive oil in a frying pan over medium heat. Add the onions and garlic and fry until they're translucent (about 3–4 minutes). Add the fennel seeds, chilli flakes and half of the sage to the pan and combine. Season with salt and pepper and set this mixture aside to cool.

Add the remainder of the sage to the minced pork and season generously with salt and pepper. Gently fold the meat with your hands. Add the cooled onion mix, the eggs, breadcrumbs, orange zest and parmesan cheese, and evenly combine with your hands. Set the mixture aside in the refrigerator to cool for 30 minutes.

Preheat the oven to 160°C (315°F) and add a small ovenproof saucer of water to the back of the oven to create humidity.

Remove the cooled meatball mixture from the refrigerator and gently roll it into 60 g (2¼ oz) balls with your hands.

Spray a baking tray with olive oil and carefully place the meatballs in the tray. Cook in the oven for 16 minutes, then remove and let the balls rest in their cooking liquid until ready to serve.

Note: Don't throw away the cooking liquid left in the bottom of the baking tray – it's full of juicy pork fat and infused with the aromas of fennel, orange and sage. Use this cooking liquid instead of butter or olive oil when frying onions, or add the liquid to a stock and reduce it down to make a beautiful, fragrant and rich sauce.

Sotto palle

Creamy polenta (p 144) or
Lasagne sheets (p 146) or
Super potato smash (p 145)

Sauces

Butter & sage sauce (p 159) or
Chunky Italian red sauce (p 157) or
Italian veal jus (p 156)

Garnishes *(pp 166-9)*

Citrus zest or
Fried sage or
Toasted pistachios

GINGER, LEMONGRASS, PORK & STICKY RICE

OVEN BAKE
PAN-FRY

MAKES 60 MEATBALLS

THANKS TO THE RICE IN THIS RECIPE, THESE MEATBALLS ARE SUPER LIGHT – AND WHEN COMBINED WITH GINGER AND LEMONGRASS, THEY PACK A PUNCH ON THE FLAVOUR SCALE. MAKE A SMALL TEST BATCH AND ADJUST THE LEVELS OF CHILLI TO SUIT YOUR TASTES.

200 G (7 OZ/1 CUP) JASMINE RICE
80 ML (2½ FL OZ/⅓ CUP) FISH SAUCE
80 ML (2½ FL OZ/⅓ CUP) MIRIN (RICE WINE)
25 G (1 OZ) FINELY CHOPPED LEMONGRASS
50 G (1¾ OZ) GINGER, COARSELY CHOPPED
1 LARGE FRESH GREEN CHILLI, WITH SEEDS, COARSELY CHOPPED
1 KG (2 LB 4 OZ) MINCED (GROUND) PORK
30 G (1 OZ/1 SMALL BUNCH) CORIANDER (CILANTRO), LEAVES PICKED AND CHOPPED
ZEST OF 1 SMALL LIME
2 TABLESPOONS SOFT BROWN SUGAR
OLIVE OIL SPRAY, FOR BAKING
VEGETABLE OIL, FOR FRYING

Cook the rice following the packet directions.

Spread out the cooked rice in a baking tray, cover with the fish sauce and mirin and combine thoroughly with a fork so that the rice becomes slightly sticky. Set aside to cool.

Use a mortar and pestle to bash the lemongrass, ginger and chilli until a paste forms.

Preheat the oven to 160°C (315°F) and add a small ovenproof saucer of water to the back of the oven to create humidity.

In a mixing bowl, lightly season the pork with salt and pepper and combine with the cooled rice, the lemongrass paste, the coriander, lime zest and brown sugar. Using your hands, gently roll the mixture into 30 g (1 oz) balls.

Spray a baking tray with olive oil and carefully place the pork balls in the tray. Bake in the humid oven for 10 minutes.

Heat up a drizzle of vegetable oil in a frying pan over medium heat. Once the oil is hot, introduce the pork balls a few at a time, taking care not to overcrowd the pan. You can do this in stages. Constantly move the pan in a circling motion. This will help the balls roll around the pan and achieve a nice even colour. This should take around 2–3 minutes.

Serve while hot.

Sotto palle

Buttered edamame (p 147) or
Pea, mint & ricotta salad (p 147) or
Wasabi slaw (p 151)

Sauces

Aioli (p 160) or
Green sauce (p 164) or
Spicy hoisin sauce with ginger & garlic (p 163)

Garnishes *(pp 166-9)*

Citrus zest or
Fresh red chilli or
Thinly sliced apple

PORK, TOASTED WALNUT & HONEY

MAKES 25 MEATBALLS

VERY EASY TO MAKE, THESE DELICIOUS MEATBALLS HAVE A WONDERFUL BALANCE OF SWEETNESS AND CRUNCH, THANKS TO THE HONEYED WALNUTS. THE ORANGE ZEST WITH TARRAGON MAKES THEM EVEN MORE INTERESTING.

200 G (7 OZ) WALNUTS
120 G (4¼ OZ) HONEY
1 KG (2 LB 4 OZ) MINCED (GROUND) PORK
12 TARRAGON STALKS, PICKED AND CHOPPED
½ WHITE ONION, FINELY DICED
ZEST OF 1 ORANGE
40 G (1½ OZ/⅓ CUP) DRY BREADCRUMBS
2 EGGS
OLIVE OIL SPRAY, FOR BAKING

Start by toasting the walnuts in a dry frying pan for around 5 minutes over medium–high heat. Add the honey to the pan, ensuring all the walnuts are covered. Continue to cook until the honey begins to bubble, then remove from the heat and set aside to cool.

Once cooled, chop the walnuts into small pieces.

Preheat the oven to 160°C (315°F) and add a small ovenproof saucer of water to the back of the oven to create humidity.

In a mixing bowl, season the pork with salt and pepper. Add the tarragon, onion, orange zest, breadcrumbs, eggs and the cooled honey walnuts, and combine thoroughly. Using your hands, gently roll 60 g (2¼ oz) balls from the mixture.

Spray a baking tray with olive oil and carefully place the balls in the tray. Cook in the humid oven for 14 minutes.

Serve while hot.

Sotto palle

Grilled mushrooms with taleggio cheese (p 150) or
Lasagne sheets (p 146) or
Panzanella 📷 (p 150)

Sauces

Aioli (p 160) or
Butter & sage sauce (p 159) or
White sauce (p 158)

Garnishes *(pp 166-9)*

Citrus zest or
Micro herbs or
Toasted pistachios

PULLED PORK & BAKED APPLE

PAN-FRY

MAKES 55 MEATBALLS

TAKING ADVANTAGE OF THE MOUTH-WATERING QUALITIES OF PULLED PORK AND BAKED APPLES, THESE MEATBALLS ARE A TRUE DELIGHT. ONCE COOKED, THE JUICES FROM THE PULLED PORK RELEASE, CREATING A FLAVOUR-PACKED MEATBALL. SERVE THESE AS A CANAPÉ WITH DIPPING SAUCES.

- 600 G (1 LB 5 OZ) PORK SHOULDER
- OLIVE OIL
- APPLE CIDER VINEGAR
- 180 G (6 OZ) APPLES
- 300 G (10½ OZ) MINCED (GROUND) PORK
- 60 G (2¼ OZ) SMOKED ALMONDS, FINELY CHOPPED
- VEGETABLE OIL, FOR FRYING

Preheat the oven to 160°C (315°F).

In a pan, sear the piece of pork in a drizzle of olive oil over high heat. Once the pork has taken on a nice brown colour, transfer it to a deep baking tray, cover the entire piece of pork in apple cider vinegar and slow-cook it for 4 hours.

Once the pork is cooked, shred the warm meat with a fork – you should have around 420 g (14¾ oz) of cooked pork. Leave it in the refrigerator to chill. It should take approximately 1 hour to cool. You want the cooking juices to cool with the meat so that they are incorporated into the meatball. Once cooled, use a sharp knife to chop the pulled pork into tiny pieces.

Turn the oven on again and set to 120°C (235°F).

To make the baked apples, simply core the apples, slice them in half and place them in a deep baking tray. Bake in the oven for around 1 hour. If the baking tray isn't non-stick, remember to grease the tray with butter. The apples will soften up and become nice and sweet. Finely chop them and set them aside to cool.

Season the pork with salt and pepper and combine with the pulled pork, baked apple and almonds in a large mixing bowl. Roll the mixture into small 15 g (½ oz) balls.

Heat up a drizzle of vegetable oil in a frying pan over medium heat. Once the oil is hot, introduce the pork balls a few at a time, taking care not to overcrowd the pan. You can do this in stages. Constantly move the pan in a circling motion. This will help the balls roll around the pan and achieve a nice even colour. This should take around 4–6 minutes.

Serve with dipping sauces while hot.

Sauces

Barbecue sauce (p 161) or
Green sauce 📷 (p 164) or
Horseradish cream (p 162)

Garnishes (pp 166-9)

Citrus zest or
Salt flakes 📷 or
Thinly sliced apple 📷

HAM MEATBALLS

MAKES *50* MEATBALLS

AN ABSOLUTE WINNER, THIS HAM VARIETY IS ANOTHER GREAT EXAMPLE OF HOW TO COMBINE YOUR FAVOURITE INGREDIENTS INTO A MEATBALL. SMOKED HAM IS THE MAIN COMPONENT HERE, BUT THE MEATBALL IS BOUND TOGETHER WITH MINCED (GROUND) PORK.

600 G (1 LB 5 OZ) HAM
300 G (10½ OZ) MINCED (GROUND) PORK
50 G (1¾ OZ/1 LARGE BUNCH) FLAT-LEAF (ITALIAN) PARSLEY, LEAVES PICKED AND FINELY CHOPPED
2 EGGS
35 G (1¼ OZ/⅓ CUP) FINELY GRATED PARMESAN CHEESE
100 G (3½ OZ) QUINCE PASTE
1 TEASPOON DIJON MUSTARD
40 G (1½ OZ/⅓ CUP) DRY BREADCRUMBS, PLUS EXTRA FOR COATING
VEGETABLE OIL, FOR FRYING

Finely chop the ham by hand with a knife or blitz it into very small pieces in a food processor.

In a mixing bowl, season the pork with salt and pepper. Add the remaining ingredients and combine. Using your hands, gently roll the mixture into 25 g (1 oz) balls, and roll them through the extra breadcrumbs to coat.

Preheat the oven to 125°C (250°F).

Heat up a drizzle of vegetable oil in a frying pan over medium heat. Once the oil is hot, introduce the pork balls a few at a time, taking care not to overcrowd the pan. You can do this in stages. Constantly move the pan in a circling motion. This will help the balls roll around the pan until a nice golden crust has formed. This should take around 3–4 minutes.

Spray a baking tray with olive oil and carefully place the balls in the tray. Bake in the dry oven for 8 minutes.

Serve while hot.

Sotto palle

Cheesy bread (p 153) or
Creamy polenta (p 144) or
Roasted fennel with almond & lemon butter crumb (p 153)

Sauces

Aioli (p 160) or
Napoli cruda (p 165) or
White sauce (p 158)

Garnishes *(pp 166-9)*

Chilli oil or
Cracked black pepper or
Salt flakes

SAUSAGE – THE CHEAT'S MEATBALL

PAN-FRY

MAKES **55** MEATBALLS

A QUICK AND EASY WAY TO MAKE MEATBALLS IS TO UTILISE EXISTING SAUSAGE MEAT AND RE-FORM IT INTO BALLS. YOU CAN USE ANY VARIETY OF SAUSAGE – WHATEVER YOU FEEL LIKE ON THE DAY. THE SAUSAGE INGREDIENTS AND BINDING AGENTS ARE PERFECT FOR GRILLING.

350 G (12 OZ) OF YOUR FAVOURITE SAUSAGES (ABOUT 5)
350 G (12 OZ) MINCED (GROUND) PORK
100 G (3½ OZ) FETA CHEESE, CUT INTO CUBES
FRESH HERBS (ANY VARIETY, LEAVES PICKED AND CHOPPED)
OLIVE OIL

Remove the sausage filling from the casings and break the meat apart with your hands.

In a mixing bowl, season the minced pork with salt and pepper, add the feta cheese and fresh herbs, and mix everything together with the sausage meat. Roll the mixture into 20 g (¾ oz) balls with your hands.

Pour a good drizzle of olive oil into a frying pan and place the pan over medium–high heat. Once the oil is hot, add the meatballs, taking care not to overcrowd the pan. You can do this in stages. Constantly move the pan in a circling motion. This will help the balls roll around the pan and brown evenly. Do this for around 6 minutes until the balls are golden on all sides.

Serve immediately.

Sotto palle

Cheesy bread (p 153) or
Grilled mushrooms with taleggio cheese (p 150) or
Wasabi slaw (p 151)

Sauces

Aioli (p 160) or
Barbecue sauce (p 161) or
Hot tomato & eggplant sauce (p 161)

Garnishes *(pp 166-9)*

Citrus zest or
Grated cheese or
Salt flakes

LAGER

SALAMI MEATBALLS

MAKES 24 MEATBALLS

SALAMI AND OTHER CURED MEAT PRODUCTS ARE SENSATIONAL INGREDIENTS TO ADD TO MEATBALLS. THE TRICK WITH USING CURED MEATS IS TO ENSURE THAT YOU CUT THEM DOWN TO THE VERY TINIEST SIZE BEFORE ADDING THEM TO THE MINCED (GROUND) MEAT. IF YOU INTRODUCE LARGE PIECES OF CURED MEATS INTO YOUR MEATBALLS, IT'S LIKELY THEY WILL BECOME TOUGH AND RUBBERY DURING THE COOKING PROCESS AND SPOIL THE QUALITY OF THE DISH. ONCE INTRODUCED INTO YOUR MEATBALL RECIPES, CURED MEATS AND ALL THEIR SALTY GOODNESS ENSURE A TRULY WONDERFUL MEATBALL EXPERIENCE.

- 800 G (1 LB 12 OZ) MINCED (GROUND) PORK
- 200 G (7 OZ) SALAMI, FINELY DICED OR BLITZED
- 1 TEASPOON CHILLI FLAKES
- 100 G (3½ OZ) RED ONION, FINELY DICED
- 2 GARLIC CLOVES, FINELY DICED
- 2 EGGS
- 90 G (3¼ OZ/¾ CUP) DRY BREADCRUMBS
- 100 G (3½ OZ) CHUNKY ITALIAN RED SAUCE (P 157)
- 50 G (1¾ OZ/½ CUP) FINELY GRATED PARMESAN CHEESE
- 1½ TEASPOONS CUMIN POWDER
- 1½ TEASPOONS SMOKED PAPRIKA
- 25 G (1 OZ) KALAMATA OLIVES, DICED
- 60 ML (2 FL OZ/¼ CUP) OLIVE OIL
- 30 G (1 OZ/1 SMALL BUNCH) BASIL, LEAVES PICKED AND CHOPPED
- 10 OREGANO SPRIGS, LEAVES PICKED AND CHOPPED
- OLIVE OIL, FOR FRYING

In a mixing bowl, season the pork with salt and pepper, and add all the other ingredients. Gently fold everything together with your hands. Roll the mixture into 60 g (2¼ oz) portions and set them aside.

Preheat the oven to 120°C (235°F).

Heat up a good drizzle of olive oil in an ovenproof frying pan over medium–high heat. Once the oil is hot, add the meatballs, taking care not to overcrowd the pan. You can do this in stages. Constantly move the pan in a circling motion. This will help the balls roll around and sear evenly. Do this for several minutes until the balls are nice and golden all the way around.

Once they're all golden, return all meatballs to the pan and transfer it to the oven for 8 minutes to finish the cooking process.

Serve while still hot.

Note: The best way to get the ends of salami and prosciutto into small pieces is to chill the cured meats and then blitz them in a powerful food processor. This is, of course, much easier if the cured meats are already sliced. Alternatively, you can pass the cured meats through the finest mince plate on your meat grinder.

Sotto palle

Cheesy bread (p 153) or
Lasagne sheets (p 146) or
Super potato smash (p 145)

Sauces

Chunky Italian red sauce (p 157) or
Horseradish cream (p 162) or
Labna (p 157)

Garnishes (pp 166-9)

Citrus zest or
Fried sage or
Grated cheese

HONEY-GLAZED CHICKEN

DEEP-FRY

MAKES *38* MEATBALLS

Although these tasty morsels require slightly more work than regular meatballs, they are a delight, with a sweet outer crumb and delicate and soft centre.

- 60 G (2¼ OZ) BUTTER
- 1 MEDIUM LEEK, PALE PART ONLY, FINELY CHOPPED
- 1 KG (2 LB 4 OZ) MINCED (GROUND) CHICKEN THIGH
- ZEST OF 2 LEMONS
- 1 TABLESPOON SWEET CHILLI SAUCE
- 30 G (1 OZ/¼ CUP) DRY BREADCRUMBS
- 2 EGGS
- 1 HANDFUL CORIANDER (CILANTRO) LEAVES, CHOPPED
- 200 G (7 OZ) HONEY, PLUS EXTRA FOR DRIZZLING (OPTIONAL)
- 40 G (1½ OZ/¼ CUP) SESAME SEEDS
- 100 G (3½ OZ/1⅔ CUPS) PANKO (JAPANESE-STYLE) BREADCRUMBS
- VEGETABLE OIL, FOR FRYING

Heat up the butter in a frying pan over low–medium heat, add the chopped leek and cook until translucent (about 4–6 minutes). Set aside in the refrigerator to cool.

In a mixing bowl, season the minced chicken with salt and pepper, add the chilled leek, lemon zest, sweet chilli sauce, dry breadcrumbs, eggs and coriander. Mix everything together, taking care to be as gentle as possible. Using your hands, roll the mixture into 40 g (1½ oz) balls and place them on a tray and into the refrigerator for at least 45 minutes. Always take care to ensure your hands and all surfaces that are in contact with the chicken are properly cleaned and sanitised after each action.

Heat up the honey until runny and place it into a shallow bowl. In a separate bowl, add the sesame seeds and the panko crumbs, and season with salt and pepper. Take the chilled chicken balls from the refrigerator. Coat them in honey one by one, then roll them around in the seasoned panko and sesame mix. Repeat this process until you are satisfied you have created a nice outer crumb. You may need to re-form the balls with your cupped hands if they start to lose their shape. Do this with all the balls and place them back in the refrigerator to remain cool.

Pour vegetable oil into a stockpot until it's at least half full and place over a controlled medium–high heat until the oil reaches approximately 160–180°C (315–350°F). The oil is ready when breadcrumbs sizzle but do not burn when added to the oil. Once it's the correct temperature, drop in a few balls, one at a time, and cook until golden. This should take around 6 minutes. Carefully take one ball out and cut it in half to ensure it's cooked all the way through. Once you are satisfied all the meatballs are cooked, carefully remove them from the oil and place them on paper towel to absorb any excess oil.

Serve immediately.

Optional: Drizzle a little bit of honey over the hot balls before serving for extra sweetness.

Sotto palle

Buttered edamame (p 147) or
Buttered risoni & peas (p 144) or
Wasabi slaw (p 151)

Sauces

Aioli (p 160) or
Labna (p 157) or
Sofritto (p 159)

Garnishes *(pp 166-9)*

Citrus zest or
Micro herbs or
Parmesan crisps

CHICKEN, PISTACHIO & MUSCATEL

OVEN BAKE

MAKES 22 MEATBALLS

ALWAYS A CROWD-PLEASER, THESE DELICIOUS CHICKEN BALLS FEATURE THE CRUNCH OF PISTACHIOS AND THE DELICATE SWEETNESS OF MUSCATELS. CHICKEN BINDS FAIRLY WELL, SO THE FINAL TEXTURE OF THIS BALL FEELS SOMEWHAT LIKE A TERRINE. YOU CAN MODIFY THIS RECIPE BY ADDING MORE OR LESS OF ANY OF THE INGREDIENTS TO SUIT YOUR TASTE.

1 KG (2 LB 4 OZ) MINCED (GROUND) CHICKEN THIGH
60 G (2¼ OZ) PISTACHIO NUTS, COARSELY CHOPPED
45 G (1½ OZ/¼ CUP) MUSCATELS, CHOPPED
ZEST OF 1 LEMON
90 G (3¼ OZ) BUTTER, SOFTENED
90 G (3¼ OZ/¾ CUP) DRY BREADCRUMBS
1 PINCH GROUND NUTMEG
1 EGG
50 G (1¾ OZ/½ CUP) FINELY GRATED PARMESAN CHEESE
OLIVE OIL SPRAY, FOR BAKING

Preheat the oven to 160°C (315°F) and add a small ovenproof saucer of water to the back of the oven to create humidity.

In a mixing bowl, gently combine all of the ingredients with your hands. Using your hands, gently roll the mixture into 60 g (2¼ oz) balls.

Spray a baking tray with olive oil and carefully place the meatballs into the tray. Bake in the humid oven for 14 minutes.

Serve while hot.

Sotto palle

Buttered edamame (p 147) or
Lasagne sheets (p 146) or
Pea, mint & ricotta salad (p 147)

Sauces

Aioli (p 160) or
Green sauce (p 164) or
White sauce (p 158)

Garnishes *(pp 166-9)*

Citrus zest or
Fresh herbs or
Toasted pistachios

MORTADELLA & BREAD WITH CHICKEN & PORK

POACH

MAKES *100* MEATBALLS

Mortadella is an Italian pork product, which is unctuous and rich. It's a key ingredient here, along with lots of bread, which makes these meatballs perfect for poaching in a stock or using in soups. It's the ultimate comfort food.

- 450 G (1 LB) SLICED WHITE BREAD, ABOUT 9 SLICES
- 250 ML (9 FL OZ/1 CUP) OLIVE OIL
- 1½ TABLESPOONS DRIED OREGANO
- 300 G (10½ OZ) SLICED MORTADELLA, COARSELY CHOPPED
- 300 G (10½ OZ) MINCED (GROUND) PORK
- 150 G (5½ OZ) MINCED (GROUND) CHICKEN THIGH
- 25 GREEN OLIVES, PITTED
- 2 SMALL EGGS
- 25 G (1 OZ/¼ CUP) FINELY GRATED PARMESAN CHEESE
- ZEST OF ½ ORANGE
- 3 TEASPOONS FRESHLY GRATED NUTMEG (1½ NUTS), PLUS EXTRA FOR SEASONING
- PISTACHIO NUTS (OPTIONAL)
- 2 LITRES (70 FL OZ/8 CUPS) CHICKEN STOCK

Preheat the oven to 120°C (235°F).

Cut the bread into 1 cm (½ in) pieces and place them in a baking tray. Toss them with the olive oil, oregano and salt and pepper. Bake them in the dry oven for around 15 minutes. Set them aside to cool.

In a food processor, add the cooled bread, the meats, olives, eggs, parmesan cheese, orange zest and nutmeg, and blitz until the mixture is completely combined. Avoid blitzing for too long, as a dough will form. Using your hands, gently roll the mixture into 10 g (¼ oz) balls. If you'd like some added texture, insert one pistachio nut into the centre of each meatball before cooking.

Pour the chicken stock into a saucepan over medium heat and bring to a gentle simmer. Add the meatballs and poach them for around 6 minutes. The balls are ready when they float to the top. Remove with a slotted spoon and serve immediately.

Optional: Grate some more fresh nutmeg over the top as desired and serve while hot.

Sotto palle

Italian beans (p 154) or
Minestrone (p 154) or
Simple mushroom risotto (p 149)

Sauces

Butter & sage sauce (p 159) or
Sofritto (p 159) or
White sauce (p 158)

Garnishes (pp 166-9)

Cracked black pepper or
Grated cheese or
Truffle salt

CHICKEN, CORN & CHEESE

MAKES *30* MEATBALLS

THE THREE C'S IN ONE AMAZING MOUTHFUL – CHICKEN, CORN AND CHEESE – A WINNING COMBINATION. USE YOUR FAVOURITE CHEESE IN THIS RECIPE TO MAKE IT YOUR OWN. HERE, WE'VE USED AGED CHEDDAR FOR ITS SHARPNESS.

2 CORN COBS
80 G (2¾ OZ) CORNFLAKES
100 G (3½ OZ) SALT-REDUCED BUTTER, PLUS EXTRA FOR FRYING
500 G (1 LB 2 OZ) MINCED (GROUND) CHICKEN THIGH
150 G (5½ OZ/1½ CUPS) CHEDDAR CHEESE, GRATED
1 SPRING ONION (SCALLION), FINELY DICED
ZEST OF 1 SMALL LEMON
30 G (1 OZ/1 SMALL BUNCH) FLAT-LEAF (ITALIAN) PARSLEY, LEAVES PICKED AND CHOPPED
160 G (5½ OZ/⅔ CUP) CREAMED CORN
3 TABLESPOONS JAPANESE MAYONNAISE
OLIVE OIL SPRAY, FOR BAKING
OLIVE OIL

Char the corn cobs on a hotplate or barbecue plate, turning a few times, until cooked on all sides (about 12 minutes). Set aside to cool. Once cooled, remove the kernels by slicing down the cob with a sharp blade. You should have 150 g (5½ oz) of charred corn kernels.

Crush the cornflakes into tiny pieces using a mortar and pestle. In a dry frying pan over medium heat, toast the cornflakes. Before they start to brown, add the butter and stir through until it begins to bubble. Remove from the heat and set aside in the refrigerator to cool for about 45 minutes.

In a mixing bowl, season the chicken with salt and pepper and combine with the charred corn, cornflakes, cheddar cheese, spring onion, lemon zest, parsley, creamed corn and mayonnaise. Cool the mixture in the refrigerator for at least 30 minutes.

Preheat the oven to 120°C (235°F) and add a small ovenproof saucer of water to the back of the oven to create humidity.

Retrieve the cooled mixture from the refrigerator. Using your hands, gently roll the mixture into 40 g (1½ oz) balls.

Spray a baking tray with olive oil and carefully place the meatballs in the tray. Bake the meatballs in the humid oven for 12 minutes.

Heat up a knob of butter and a drizzle of olive oil in a frying pan over medium heat. Take the meatballs out of the oven and finish them in the pan for around 3 minutes on each side until golden brown.

Serve immediately.

Sotto palle

Buttered risoni & peas (p 144) or
Couscous with muscatels & pistachios (p 148) or
Toasted quinoa, lentils & corn (p 152)

Sauces

Aioli (p 160) or
Spicy hoisin sauce with ginger & garlic (p 163) or
White sauce (p 158)

Garnishes *(pp 166-9)*

Citrus zest or
Grated cheese or
Pickled zucchini

SPICED TURKEY MEATBALLS

MAKES 24 MEATBALLS

A WONDERFUL MIX OF SPICES AND HERBS GIVE THESE TURKEY BALLS PLENTY OF DEPTH, WHILE THE TURKEY MEAT ENSURES THEY'RE INCREDIBLY LEAN AND HEALTHY. THOUGH OVEN-BAKED, THEY'RE FINISHED OFF IN THE PAN TO ENSURE A LOVELY GOLDEN CRUST.

- 1 KG (2 LB 4 OZ) MINCED (GROUND) TURKEY
- 2½ TABLESPOONS OLIVE OIL, PLUS EXTRA FOR FRYING
- 100 G (3½ OZ) RED ONION, FINELY DICED
- 2 GARLIC CLOVES, FINELY DICED
- 1 SMALL HANDFUL OREGANO, LEAVES PICKED AND CHOPPED
- 1 SMALL HANDFUL BASIL, LEAVES PICKED AND CHOPPED
- 1 TEASPOON CHILLI FLAKES, ADD MORE OR LESS DEPENDING ON PREFERENCE
- 1 PINCH CAYENNE PEPPER
- 2 TEASPOONS CUMIN POWDER
- 1 TEASPOON SMOKED PAPRIKA
- 1 TABLESPOON FRESHLY CHOPPED THYME
- 100 G (3½ OZ) CHUNKY ITALIAN RED SAUCE (P 157)
- 90 G (3¼ OZ/¾ CUP) DRY BREADCRUMBS
- 1 EGG
- 50 G (1¾ OZ) FINELY GRATED PARMESAN CHEESE
- OLIVE OIL SPRAY, FOR BAKING

In a mixing bowl, season the turkey with salt and pepper. Add the remaining ingredients and thoroughly combine. Using your hands, gently roll the mixture into 60 g (2¼ oz) balls.

Preheat the oven to 160°C (315°F) and add a small ovenproof saucer of water to the back of the oven to create humidity.

Spray a baking tray with olive oil and carefully place the balls in the tray. Bake in the humid oven for around 8–10 minutes.

Heat up a drizzle of olive oil in a frying pan. Finish the meatballs by searing them in the hot pan for a few minutes to give them some colour and to ensure they're cooked all the way through.

Sotto palle

Cheesy bread (p 153) or
Couscous with muscatels & pistachios (p 148) or
Roasted pumpkin (p 152)

Sauces

Aioli (p 160) or
Barbecue sauce (p 161) or
White sauce (p 158)

Garnishes (pp 166-9)

Grated cheese or
Hazelnut pangrattato or
Micro herbs

TURKEY, QUINOA & PEA

OVEN BAKE

MAKES 20 MEATBALLS

QUINOA IS A FANTASTIC INGREDIENT TO USE IN MEATBALLS AND WHEN COMBINED WITH A LEAN MEAT LIKE MINCED TURKEY, THE RESULT IS A WONDERFULLY LIGHT, TEXTURED AND HEALTHY MEATBALL.

- 100 G (3½ OZ/½ CUP) QUINOA
- 500 G (1 LB 2 OZ) MINCED (GROUND) TURKEY
- 130 G (4½ OZ/1 CUP) FROZEN PEAS, COOKED AND SMASHED
- 60 G (2¼ OZ/1 CUP) PANKO (JAPANESE-STYLE) BREADCRUMBS
- 2½ TABLESPOONS EXTRA VIRGIN OLIVE OIL
- 1 EGG, WHISKED
- 2 GARLIC CLOVES, CRUSHED
- ½ SMALL ONION, THINLY SLICED
- 1 PINCH GROUND GINGER
- ¼ TEASPOON CHILLI POWDER (OPTIONAL)
- OLIVE OIL SPRAY, FOR BAKING

Cook the quinoa following the packet directions.

Preheat the oven to 160°C (315°F).

Gently combine all of the ingredients together in a mixing bowl and season with salt and pepper. Using your hands, roll 50 g (1¾ oz) balls from the mixture.

Carefully place the balls in a baking tray and spray them with olive oil.

Bake in the dry oven for 10–12 minutes until cooked through.

Serve while hot.

Note: Add chilli powder to the mixture before rolling the meatballs if you're after some heat.

Sotto palle

Buttered risoni & peas (p 144) or
Roasted pumpkin (p 152) or
Toasted quinoa, lentils & corn (p 152)

Sauces

Butter & sage sauce 📷 (p 159) or
Labna (p 157) or
Sofritto (p 159)

Garnishes *(pp 166-9)*

Citrus zest or
Parmesan crisps or
Toasted pistachios

TURKEY & CRANBERRY

OVEN BAKE
PAN-FRY

MAKES 35 MEATBALLS

Wonderfully lean minced turkey makes a rich and delectable meatball when matched with classic accompanying ingredients, such as sweet cranberry sauce and creamy camembert cheese.

- 150 G (5½ OZ) BUTTER
- OLIVE OIL
- 240 G (8½ OZ) LEEKS, PALE PART ONLY, FINELY CHOPPED
- 300 G (10½ OZ) CRANBERRY SAUCE
- 240 G (8½ OZ) SOFT WHITE SLICED BREAD, CUT INTO 1 CM (½ IN) CUBES
- 750 G (1 LB 10 OZ) MINCED (GROUND) TURKEY
- 40 G (1½ OZ/¼ CUP) SWEETENED DRIED CRANBERRIES
- 15 LARGE BASIL LEAVES, CHOPPED
- 150 G (5½ OZ) CAMEMBERT CHEESE, CUT INTO ½ CM (¼ IN) CUBES
- OLIVE OIL SPRAY, FOR BAKING

Heat up the butter and a drizzle of olive oil in a frying pan, add the leek and cook over medium heat until softened (about 3–4 minutes). Season with salt and pepper. Once the leeks are cooked, add the cranberry sauce and stir through.

Add the soft white bread to the pan to soak up all the juices. Remove the mixture from the pan and set aside to cool. Keep the pan and the residual cooking juices handy as it will be used later to cook the meatballs.

In a mixing bowl, season the turkey with salt and pepper, and add the dried cranberries and basil. Add the cooled leek, cranberry and bread mix, and combine thoroughly.

Preheat the oven to 120°C (235°F) and add a small ovenproof saucer of water to the back of the oven to create humidity.

Using your hands, gently roll the turkey mixture into 50 g (1¾ oz) balls. Use your thumb to create a well in a ball and insert a cube of camembert cheese, re-forming the ball around it. Repeat with the other balls.

Spray a baking tray with olive oil and carefully place the balls in the tray. Cook the balls in the humid oven for 16 minutes.

To finish off the balls, pour a drizzle of olive oil into the original frying pan and set over medium heat. Once the oil is hot, introduce the turkey balls a few at a time, taking care not to overcrowd the pan. You can do this in stages. Constantly move the pan in a circling motion. This will help the balls roll around the pan and achieve a nice even colour. This should take about 2 minutes.

It's important to serve these balls immediately so the camembert cheese remains melted.

Sotto palle

Cheesy bread (p 153) or
Couscous with muscatels & pistachios (p 148) or
Roasted pumpkin (p 152)

Sauces

Aioli (p 160) or
Barbecue sauce (p 161) or
White sauce (p 158)

Garnishes *(pp 166-9)*

Cracked black pepper 📷 or
Hazelnut pangrattato or
Toasted pistachios

DUCK MEATBALLS

OVEN BAKE

MAKES 24 MEATBALLS

DUCK HAS A VERY DISTINCT, DELICIOUS FLAVOUR AND WHEN MINCED, HAS A WONDERFULLY SOFT AND RICH TEXTURE. HERE WE'VE COMBINED THE DUCK WITH SOME PORK FAT TO MAINTAIN MOISTURE IN THE BALL.

1½ SLICES DAY-OLD WHITE BREAD
170 ML (5½ FL OZ/⅔ CUP) MILK
900 G (2 LB) MINCED (GROUND) DUCK
100 G (3½ OZ) MINCED (GROUND) PORK FAT
2 EGGS
1 TEASPOON FENNEL SEEDS
1½ TEASPOONS CHOPPED TARRAGON LEAVES
2 GARLIC CLOVES, FINELY GRATED
35 G (1¼ OZ/⅓ CUP) FINELY GRATED PARMESAN CHEESE
OLIVE OIL SPRAY, FOR BAKING

Preheat the oven to 160°C (315°F) and add a small ovenproof saucer of water to the back of the oven to create humidity.

Soak the bread in the milk and strain off the excess milk by squeezing the bread with your hands. Tear up the bread into small pieces.

Season the duck with salt and pepper and combine all of the ingredients together. Using your hands, gently roll the mixture into 50 g (1¾ oz) balls.

Spray a baking tray with olive oil and carefully place the balls in the tray. Cook in the humid oven for 14 minutes.

Serve immediately.

Sotto palle

Buttered risoni & peas (p 144) or
Creamy polenta (p 144) or
Lasagne sheets (p 146)

Sauces

Butter & sage sauce (p 159) or
Chunky Italian red sauce (p 157) or
Sofritto (p 159)

Garnishes (pp 166-9)

Edible flowers or
Herb oil or
Micro herbs

RABBIT MEATBALLS

OVEN BAKE

MAKES 22 MEATBALLS

RABBIT IS WIDELY USED ACROSS EUROPE AND IT'S READILY AVAILABLE FROM ALMOST ANY BUTCHER SHOP IN AUSTRALIA. RABBIT MEAT IS VERY LEAN AND TENDS TO BECOME DRY IF OVERCOOKED. THIS RECIPE COMBINES RABBIT WITH SOME CHICKEN THIGH TO HELP MAINTAIN MOISTURE IN THE BALL.

- 5 DRIED FIGS, CHOPPED
- 100 ML (3½ FL OZ) BRANDY
- 20 G (¾ OZ) BUTTER
- 1 SMALL ONION, DICED
- 2 GARLIC CLOVES, FINELY DICED
- 60 ML (2 FL OZ/¼ CUP) SWEET SHERRY
- 500 G (1 LB 2 OZ) COARSELY MINCED (GROUND) RABBIT LEG
- 500 G (1 LB 2 OZ) MINCED (GROUND) CHICKEN THIGH
- 2 EGGS, WHISKED
- 50 G (1¾ OZ/½ CUP) FINELY GRATED PECORINO CHEESE
- 3 TABLESPOONS FRESHLY CHOPPED TARRAGON
- ZEST OF ½ LEMON
- 40 G (1½ OZ/⅓ CUP) DRY BREADCRUMBS
- SALT FLAKES
- OLIVE OIL SPRAY, FOR BAKING

Place the figs in a bowl and cover them with the brandy. Sit them in the fridge overnight (or for a minimum of 3–5 hours) to macerate, or soften. Strain the liquid and reserve the figs.

Warm up the butter in a frying pan over medium heat. Add the onion and garlic and cook for about 4–6 minutes until softened. Then, add the sherry and cook until it has reduced by half. This should take about 4 minutes.

Put the onion, garlic and sherry mixture in a bowl and place in the refrigerator for about 1 hour. Chill completely before adding the figs, the meats, egg, pecorino cheese, tarragon, lemon zest and breadcrumbs. Season well with salt flakes and freshly ground white pepper. Refrigerate the mixture for 30 minutes.

Preheat the oven to 160°C (315°F) and add a small ovenproof saucer of water to the back of the oven to create humidity.

Remove the chilled mixture from the refrigerator and, using your hands, gently roll the mixture into 60 g (2¼ oz) balls.

Spray a baking tray with olive oil spray and bake in the humid oven for 12–14 minutes.

Serve immediately.

Sotto palle

Buttered risoni & peas (p 144) or
Grilled mushrooms with taleggio cheese (p 150) or
Roasted fennel with almond & lemon butter crumb (p 153)

Sauces

Chunky Italian red sauce (p 157) or
Italian veal jus (p 156) or
Sofritto (p 159)

Garnishes (pp 166-9)

Citrus zest or
Fried sage or
Salt flakes

KANGAROO MEATBALLS

SHALLOW-FRY
OVEN BAKE

MAKES 45 MEATBALLS

KANGAROO IS A WONDERFULLY LEAN AND NUTRIENT-RICH PROTEIN TO EAT. IT HAS A DISTINCT FLAVOUR, WHICH COMBINES WELL WITH OTHER STRONG AROMATICS, SUCH AS ROSEMARY, CURRANTS AND POMEGRANATE.

½ WHITE BREAD SLICE
2½ TABLESPOONS MILK
1 KG (2 LB 4 OZ) MINCED (GROUND) KANGAROO
2 TEASPOONS POMEGRANATE GLAZE
2 TABLESPOONS CURRANTS
30 G (1 OZ/1 SMALL BUNCH) ROSEMARY, LEAVES PICKED AND FINELY CHOPPED
30 G (1 OZ/1 SMALL BUNCH) FLAT-LEAF (ITALIAN) PARSLEY, LEAVES PICKED AND FINELY CHOPPED
1 SMALL CARROT, GRATED
1 GARLIC CLOVE, FINELY DICED
1 EGG
30 G (1 OZ/¼ CUP) DRY BREADCRUMBS
VEGETABLE OIL, FOR FRYING

Soak the bread in the milk and strain off the excess milk by squeezing the bread with your hands. Tear up the bread into small pieces.

Season the kangaroo with salt and pepper in a mixing bowl, add all of the ingredients and combine well. Set the mixture aside to cool in the refrigerator for 30 minutes.

Preheat the oven to 160°C (315°F) and add a small ovenproof saucer of water to the back of the oven to create humidity.

Remove the mixture from the refrigerator and gently roll 25 g (1 oz) balls with your hands.

Pour vegetable oil into an ovenproof frying pan until it's 1–3 cm (½–1¼ in) deep, and place over medium heat until the oil is hot. Shallow-fry the meatballs in the pan for 2–3 minutes, turning them over to create a nice even colour. Transfer the pan to the humid oven and bake for 6 minutes.

Serve immediately.

Note: You can buy pomegranate glaze (or pomegranate molasses or syrup) at any good grocery store.

Sotto palle

Grilled mushrooms with taleggio cheese (p 150) or
Super potato smash (p 145) or
Toasted quinoa, lentils & corn (p 152)

Sauces

Barbecue sauce (p 161) or
Chunky Italian red sauce (p 157) or
Hot tomato & eggplant sauce (p 161)

Garnishes *(pp 166-9)*

Citrus zest or
Fresh herbs or
Salt flakes

WILD BOAR

OVEN BAKE

MAKES 24 MEATBALLS

YOU'LL NEED TO ASK YOUR BUTCHER FOR THIS. WILD BOAR HAS A WONDERFULLY DISTINCT FLAVOUR, SLIGHTLY STRONGER AND GAMIER THAN REGULAR PORK. THIS RECIPE COMBINES WILD BOAR WITH A SMALL AMOUNT OF BEEF TO GIVE THESE MEATBALLS GREAT TEXTURE AND A BALANCE OF MEATY GOODNESS.

- 50 G (1¾ OZ) BUTTER
- 1 ONION, FINELY DICED
- 1 APPLE, DICED
- 800 G (1 LB 12 OZ) MINCED (GROUND) WILD BOAR
- 200 G (7 OZ) MINCED (GROUND) BEEF
- 3 GARLIC CLOVES, CRUSHED
- 6 ROSEMARY SPRIGS, LEAVES PICKED AND CHOPPED
- 1 TABLESPOON MUSTARD
- 150 G (5½ OZ) CHUNKY ITALIAN RED SAUCE (P 157)
- 2 EGGS
- 40 G (1½ OZ/⅓ CUP) DRY BREADCRUMBS
- OLIVE OIL SPRAY, FOR BAKING

Melt the butter in a frying pan over low heat and cook the onion for about 4–6 minutes until soft. Add the apple and cook for around 6 minutes, until the apple is soft but not too mushy. Remove and set aside to cool.

Preheat the oven to 160°C (315°F) and add a small ovenproof saucer of water to the back of the oven to create humidity.

In a mixing bowl, season the wild boar and beef with salt and pepper. Add the remaining ingredients and gently combine with your hands. Roll the mixture into 60 g (2¼ oz) balls.

Spray a baking tray with olive oil and carefully place the balls in the tray. Bake in the humid oven for 14 minutes.

Serve while hot.

Sotto palle

Creamy polenta (p 144) or
Simple mushroom risotto (p 149) or
Super potato smash (p 145)

Sauces

Chunky Italian red sauce (p 157) or
Creamy mushroom sauce 📷 (p 164) or
Red wine & onion sauce (p 162)

Garnishes *(pp 166-9)*

Fresh herbs 📷 or
Fresh red chilli or
Grated cheese 📷

GOAT MEATBALLS

PAN-FRY

MAKES 32 MEATBALLS

GOAT IS A WONDERFUL PROTEIN TO WORK WITH AND IS GENERALLY USED IN SLOW-COOKED RECIPES, DUE TO ITS LEAN MUSCLE PROFILE. WHEN MINCED, GOAT MEAT CAN BE COOKED AT HIGHER TEMPERATURES OVER A SHORTER PERIOD, MAKING IT AN IDEAL OPTION FOR MEATBALLS. ASK YOUR BUTCHER TO MINCE THE MEAT FROM THE GOAT LEG FOR THIS RECIPE.

- OLIVE OIL
- 20 G (3/4 OZ) BUTTER
- 1 LARGE ONION, FINELY CHOPPED
- 3 GARLIC CLOVES, CRUSHED
- 1 KG (2 LB 4 OZ) MINCED (GROUND) GOAT LEG
- 3 TABLESPOONS FINELY CHOPPED SAGE LEAVES
- 3 TABLESPOONS FINELY CHOPPED ROSEMARY
- 2 EGG YOLKS
- 2 TEASPOONS DOLMA SPICE (EQUAL QUANTITIES OF GROUND CINNAMON, CLOVES, NUTMEG, ALLSPICE)
- 2 TABLESPOONS PLAIN (ALL-PURPOSE) FLOUR

Heat a generous drizzle of olive oil and the butter in a frying pan over low–medium heat. Add the onion and garlic and cook until translucent (about 10 minutes). Set aside to cool.

Season the goat with salt and pepper, and combine with the cooled onion and garlic, and the remaining ingredients. Mix thoroughly and roll the mixture into 40 g (1 1/2 oz) balls.

Heat up a generous drizzle of olive oil in a frying pan over medium–high heat. Once the oil is hot, add the meatballs, taking care not to overcrowd the pan. You can do this in stages. Constantly move the pan in a circling motion. This will help the balls roll around the pan and brown evenly. Do this for around 7 minutes or until they develop a nice colour on all sides.

Serve immediately.

Sotto palle

Basic peperonata (p 151) or
Couscous with muscatels & pistachios 📷 (p 148) or
Grilled mushrooms with taleggio cheese (p 150)

Sauces

Horseradish cream (p 162) or
Italian veal jus (p 156) or
Red wine & onion sauce 📷 (p 162)

Garnishes *(pp 166-9)*

Fresh herbs 📷 or
Salt flakes 📷 or
Toasted pistachios 📷

GNOCCHI MEATBALLS

POACH

MAKES *16* MEATBALLS

SOFT PILLOWS OF DELIGHT – YES, WE'RE TALKING ABOUT GNOCCHI. THIS DISH INCORPORATES MEATBALLS WITH GNOCCHI BY INSERTING A JUICY MEATBALL INSIDE A BALL OF GNOCCHI. THE RESULTS ARE AMAZING.

GNOCCHI

750 G (1 LB 10 OZ) ALL-PURPOSE POTATOES, PEELED AND HALVED
225 G (8 OZ/1½ CUPS) PLAIN (ALL-PURPOSE) FLOUR
3 EGGS
2 TEASPOONS FRESHLY GRATED NUTMEG

MEATBALLS

325 G (11½ OZ), OR APPROXIMATELY ⅓ OF YOUR FAVOURITE MEATBALL RECIPE, UNCOOKED

Place the potatoes in lightly salted water in a large saucepan over medium–high heat and bring to the boil. Reduce the heat and cook for around 15 minutes, or until tender all the way through. If a fork penetrates easily through the potato, you'll know they are cooked. Drain the potatoes.

Meanwhile, prepare the meatball mixture according to the recipe instructions, up to the step of balling them. Divide into 15–20 g (½–¾ oz) portions and form 16 meatballs.

To make the gnocchi, pass the cooked potato through a potato ricer into a mixing bowl and add the flour, eggs, nutmeg and a generous pinch of salt. Combine thoroughly. Divide into 60 g (2¼ oz) portions and form 16 balls of gnocchi from the mixture.

Create a well in a gnocchi ball and insert a meatball. Form the gnocchi ball around the meatball. Repeat with the other gnocchi balls

Cook the meatball-stuffed gnocchi in lightly salted boiling water in a large saucepan over medium heat for around 10–12 minutes, or until the meatball inside is cooked all the way through. Carefully remove them with a slotted spoon and transfer them directly to the serving dish.

Serve while hot.

Sotto palle

Buttered edamame (p 147) or
Grilled mushrooms with taleggio cheese (p 150) or
Roasted pumpkin (p 152)

Sauces

Butter & sage sauce (p 159) or
Gorgonzola cheese sauce (p 156) or
Slow-cooked meat sauce (p 160)

Garnishes *(pp 166-9)*

Citrus zest or
Fried sage or
Salt flakes

FLAKEY FISH

MAKES 25 MEATBALLS

CREATING THESE DELICATE, FLAVOURSOME FISH BALLS IS A TWO-STEP PROCESS – THE FISH IS FIRST POACHED IN CREAM AND BUTTER AND THEN THE COOKED FISH IS TURNED INTO A BALL AND BAKED OR FRIED. IT'S AN INCREDIBLY VERSATILE RECIPE, WHERE ANY AROMATICS CAN BE ADDED TO THE POACHING LIQUID TO INFUSE INTO THE FISH. HERE, WE HAVE USED TWO FISH VARIETIES, WHICH CAN EASILY BE INTERCHANGED WITH OTHER SEASONAL FISH FROM YOUR AREA. IN GENERAL, ANY FIRM WHITE-FLESHED FISH WILL WORK WELL IN THESE FISH BALLS.

500 ML (17 FL OZ/2 CUPS) THIN (POURING) CREAM
50 G (1¾ OZ) BUTTER
2 GARLIC CLOVES, SLICED
ZEST OF 1 LEMON
2½ TABLESPOONS WHITE WINE
700 G (1 LB 9 OZ) BLUE GRENADIER FILLETS (OR BARRAMUNDI OR FLATHEAD)
300 G (10½ OZ) HAPUKA FILLETS (OR ROCKLING OR SNAPPER)
250 G (9 OZ) ALL-PURPOSE POTATOES, CHOPPED INTO SMALL CHUNKS
20 G (¾ OZ/1 SMALL BUNCH) DILL, CHOPPED
3 FRESH JALAPENO CHILLIES, FINELY DICED
30 G (1 OZ/1 SMALL BUNCH) FLAT-LEAF (ITALIAN) PARSLEY, LEAVES PICKED AND CHOPPED
OLIVE OIL SPRAY, IF BAKING
DRY BREADCRUMBS, IF FRYING
VEGETABLE OIL, IF FRYING

Warm up the cream and butter in a heavy-based stockpot over low heat, and then add the garlic and lemon zest. Add the white wine and bring the liquids to a gentle simmer. Add the fish fillets, the potato and half of the dill, and season with salt and cracked white pepper. Let the fish cook gently until it falls apart at the touch of a fork. This will take around 20 minutes, depending on the size of your fish fillets.

Take the pot off the heat, add the chillies and parsley, and set aside to rest. Use a fork to flake the fish and smash the potatoes, which by this stage should be very soft. This mixture is now fully cooked. Set it aside to cool.

Once cooled, add the remainder of the dill and season to taste. Using your hands, gently roll the mixture into 60 g (2¼ oz) balls and prepare them for cooking.

If baking, preheat the oven to 180°C (350°F). Use a half-sphere silicone baking mould (much like a muffin tray) and spray with olive oil. Place a ball in each cup, spraying the top of each ball with olive oil spray. If you don't have a silicone baking mould, a regular muffin tray will work. These balls are very delicate and the raised sides of the muffin tray will help keep them in shape. Cook them in the dry oven for 8 minutes.

If deep-frying, roll the balls in breadcrumbs first. Pour vegetable oil into a stockpot until it's at least half full and place over a controlled medium–high heat until the oil reaches approximately 160–180°C (315–350°F). The oil is ready when breadcrumbs sizzle but do not burn when added to the oil. Once it's the correct temperature, carefully drop in a few balls, one at a time, and cook until golden. This should take 3–4 minutes, or until a nice golden crust has formed around the ball. Once you are satisfied all the balls are cooked, remove them from the oil and place them on paper towel to absorb any excess oil.

Serve while hot.

Sotto palle

Fried pickled zucchini (p 148) or
Italian beans (p 154) or
Roasted fennel with almond & lemon butter crumb (p 153)

Sauces

Green sauce (p 164) or
Seafood bisque (p 165) or
Sofritto (p 159)

Garnishes *(pp 166-9)*

Fresh herbs or
Grated cheese or
Prawn oil

PRAWN BALLS

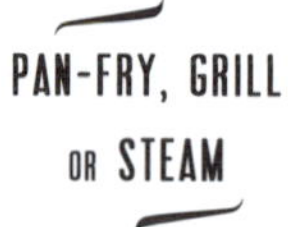

PAN-FRY, GRILL OR STEAM

MAKES 55 MEATBALLS

THESE TASTY PRAWN BALLS ARE SURPRISINGLY LIGHT AND ARE PERFECT FOR COOKING ON THE BARBECUE OR ON A HOT GRILL. THEY CAN BE SERVED ON A STICK AND DIPPED IN SAUCE OR THEY CAN ACCOMPANY A FRESH SALAD. THEY'RE ALSO PERFECT AS AN ENTRÉE OR CANAPÉ.

1 KG (2 LB 4 OZ) RAW PRAWNS (SHRIMP), PEELED AND DEVEINED
1 TABLESPOON FISH SAUCE
1 TEASPOON SUGAR
1 GARLIC CLOVE, FINELY DICED
1 FRESH RED CHILLI, FINELY DICED
1 SPRING ONION (SCALLION), FINELY DICED
30 G (1 OZ/1 SMALL BUNCH) CORIANDER (CILANTRO), LEAVES PICKED AND CHOPPED
JUICE OF ½ SMALL LIME
2 TABLESPOONS ICE-COLD WATER
DRY BREADCRUMBS (AS REQUIRED)
80 ML (2½ FL OZ/⅓ CUP) VEGETABLE OIL, IF FRYING

Gently pulse all the ingredients (except the breadcrumbs and vegetable oil) in a food processor. Do not overwork. Remove the mixture from the processor and set aside in a bowl in the refrigerator to cool for at least 1 hour.

Remove the mixture from the refrigerator and gently roll into 20 g (¾ oz) balls. If the mixture is too runny or sticky to roll into balls, introduce some breadcrumbs and stir them through the mixture until you can start to shape them into balls.

Heat up the vegetable oil in a frying pan over medium–high heat. Once the oil is hot, add the prawn balls, taking care not to overcrowd the pan. You can do this in stages. Constantly move the pan in a circling motion. This will help the balls roll around the pan and cook evenly. Do this for around 6 minutes or until golden on all sides.

Alternatively, you can cook the prawn balls on a grill or barbecue, set to high heat, for 6 minutes. It won't be possible to maintain perfectly round balls using this method, but you'll be able to create beautiful scorch marks on the sides of the prawn balls, which will add another interesting texture.

For a softer, more delicate finish, place the balls over boiling water in a steam basket for around 8–10 minutes until cooked.

Serve while hot.

Sotto palle

Fried pickled zucchini (p 148) or
Toasted quinoa, lentils & corn (p 152) or
Wasabi slaw (p 151)

Sauces

Aioli (p 160) or
Horseradish cream (p 162) or
Spicy hoisin sauce with ginger & garlic (p 163)

Garnishes *(pp 166-9)*

Chilli oil or
Fresh herbs or
Fresh red chilli

RAW TUNA

MAKES *16* MEATBALLS

USING THE VERY FINEST INGREDIENTS AVAILABLE IS ESSENTIAL WHEN CREATING THIS MEATBALL. IT'S PERFECT AS A CANAPÉ AND THE SIZE OF THE BALL CAN BE ADJUSTED TO SUIT ANY OCCASION. THESE ARE QUICK AND EASY TO MAKE AND ARE CERTAIN TO BE A HIT.

- 300 G (10½ OZ) SASHIMI-GRADE TUNA FILLET
- 2 TEASPOONS EXTRA VIRGIN OLIVE OIL
- 1 TEASPOON JAPANESE MAYONNAISE
- 2 TEASPOONS LIME JUICE
- 2 TEASPOONS LIGHT SOY SAUCE
- 15 G (½ OZ/½ SMALL BUNCH) CORIANDER (CILANTRO), LEAVES PICKED AND FINELY CHOPPED
- ½ FRESH RED CHILLI, SEEDED AND FINELY DICED
- ¼ RED ONION (OR RADISH), THINLY SLICED
- SALMON ROE (OPTIONAL)

Using a super sharp blade, delicately dice the tuna into miniature cubes and season with a touch of salt and pepper.

Combine the olive oil, Japanese mayonnaise, lime juice and light soy sauce, and add it to the diced tuna. Add the coriander, chilli and red onion, and gently fold the mixture together.

Place the mixture onto plastic wrap and tightly roll it into a sausage. Place the sausage into the refrigerator and leave for at least 1 hour to set.

When ready to serve, remove from the refrigerator and cut into 25 g (1 oz) segments. Gently roll the portions into balls and serve chilled.

Eat immediately.

Optional extra: Sprinkle some salmon roe over the top of the balls for an additional burst of flavour.

Sauces

Aioli (p 160) or
Horseradish cream (p 162) or
Spicy hoisin sauce with ginger & garlic (p 163)

Garnishes *(pp 166-9)*

Chilli oil or
Edible flowers or
Micro herbs

LOBSTER BALLS

SHALLOW-FRY

MAKES 25 MEATBALLS

Delicate, soft and decadent, these lobster balls are sure to achieve a melt-in-the-mouth moment for you and your lucky guests. It's easier to buy the lobster precooked, but if you're game, you can cook and prepare your own as well.

- 500 G (1 LB 2 OZ) LOBSTER TAIL (EITHER PRECOOKED OR 2–3 LIVE LOBSTERS, DEPENDING ON SIZE)
- 100 G (3½ OZ) ALL-PURPOSE POTATOES, CHOPPED INTO SMALL CHUNKS
- 1½ TABLESPOONS UNSALTED BUTTER
- 1¼ TABLESPOONS OLIVE OIL
- 50 G (1¾ OZ) FRENCH SHALLOT, DICED
- 1 LARGE GARLIC CLOVE, FINELY GRATED
- 2½ TABLESPOONS WHITE WINE VINEGAR
- 10 G (¼ OZ/½ BUNCH) TARRAGON, LEAVES PICKED AND CHOPPED
- 1½ TEASPOONS SALT FLAKES
- 300 G (10½ OZ) BLUE GRENADIER (OR OTHER FIRM WHITE FISH), COARSELY CHOPPED
- ZEST OF 1 LEMON
- PLAIN (ALL-PURPOSE) FLOUR, FOR COATING
- 2 EGGS, WHISKED
- DRY BREADCRUMBS, FOR COATING
- VEGETABLE OIL, FOR FRYING

If using precooked lobster, shred the lobster tail meat and set aside. If cooking the lobster yourself, place the live lobsters into a large pot of boiling water for 12–15 minutes, or until the lobster shells turn bright red. You can add aromatics to the water to create a fragrant cooking broth, such as the zest of 1 lemon, 2 dried bay leaves, sprigs of thyme and parsley and any other herbs you have in the house. Remove the cooked lobsters and separate the head from the tail by making an incision under the head with a knife and pulling the head away from the tail. Shred the lobster tail and set aside.

Cook the potatoes in lightly salted boiling water for around 12–15 minutes until tender. Drain and smash the soft potatoes with a fork, then set aside.

Prepare a beurre noisette, or browned butter, by simply bringing the butter to a gentle bubble in a frying pan over low heat and continue to cook until the butter begins to darken. This should only take 4–6 minutes. Once browned, immediately remove the butter from the heat and transfer to a chilled container.

Heat the olive oil in a frying pan over medium heat, add the shallot and garlic and cook for about 3–4 minutes. Add the white wine vinegar and reduce by half, then set aside to cool.

In a mixing bowl, combine the lobster, cooled shallot mix, potato, browned butter, tarragon, salt flakes, fish and lemon zest.

Using your hands, gently roll the mixture into 40 g (1½ oz) balls. Roll the balls in flour, then in the whisked egg, then in breadcrumbs (repeat with the egg and breadcrumbs until a thick crust has formed all the way around the ball).

Pour some vegetable oil into a deep frying pan until it's approximately 1–3 cm (½–1¼ in) deep, and place over medium–high heat. Introduce the balls a few at a time. They should start to sizzle on contact. Cook the lobster balls for around 3–4 minutes, turning them in the pan until a nice golden crust has formed.

Serve while hot.

Sotto palle

Buttered edamame (p 147) or
Buttered risoni & peas (p 144) or
Wasabi slaw (p 151)

Sauces

Aioli (p 160) or
Butter & sage sauce (p 159) or
Seafood bisque (p 165)

Garnishes (pp 166-9)

Fresh red chilli or
Micro herbs or
Prawn oil

PORK & PRAWN

PAN-FRY

MAKES 36 MEATBALLS

Panko crumbs add a wonderful crunch to the exterior of the ball, while the inside remains sweet and tangy thanks to the sugar and ginger. These pork and prawn meatballs pack some serious flavour.

2 SLICES WHITE BREAD
80 ML (2½ FL OZ/⅓ CUP) LIGHT SOY SAUCE
JUICE OF 1 LIME
2 GARLIC CLOVES
40 G (1½ OZ) GINGER, DICED
1 LARGE FRESH GREEN CHILLI, ABOUT 20 G (¾ OZ), SLICED
30 G (1 OZ/1 SMALL BUNCH) CORIANDER (CILANTRO), LEAVES PICKED
2 TEASPOONS LIGHT BROWN SUGAR
½ SPRING ONION (SCALLION), CHOPPED
300 G (10½ OZ) RAW PRAWNS (SHRIMP), PEELED AND DEVEINED
300 G (10½ OZ) MINCED (GROUND) PORK
2 EGGS
25 G (1 OZ/½ BUNCH) MINT, LEAVES PICKED AND CHOPPED
PANKO (JAPANESE-STYLE) BREADCRUMBS, FOR COATING, PLUS EXTRA IF NEEDED
VEGETABLE OIL, FOR FRYING

Soak the bread in the soy sauce and lime juice, and tear into small pieces.

Using a large mortar and pestle, bash the garlic, ginger, chilli, coriander, sugar and spring onion. Add the soaked bread and bash into a paste.

Chop up the prawns into small pieces and combine with the pork in a mixing bowl. Season with some pepper and a small amount of salt. Add the herb and bread paste, the eggs and mint, and combine thoroughly. Set the mixture aside in the refrigerator to cool for at least 45 minutes.

Once chilled, roll the mixture into 25 g (1 oz) balls. Roll the balls through panko crumbs to form a nice outer crust. If the mixture is too wet, mix through some panko crumbs until it becomes workable and less sticky.

Heat up a large drizzle of vegetable oil in a frying pan over medium heat. Once the oil is hot, introduce the balls a few at a time, taking care not to overcrowd the pan. You can do this in stages. Constantly move the pan in a circling motion. This will help the balls roll around and achieve a nice golden brown colour. This should take about 5–6 minutes.

Serve while hot.

Sotto palle

Buttered edamame (p 147) or
Fried pickled zucchini (p 148) or
Roasted pumpkin (p 152)

Sauces

Aioli (p 160) or
Barbecue sauce (p 161) or
Spicy hoisin sauce with ginger & garlic (p 163)

Garnishes *(pp 166-9)*

Chilli oil or
Hazelnut pangrattato or
Prawn oil

BAKED SEAFOOD BALLS

OVEN BAKE

MAKES *16* MEATBALLS

TO CREATE THIS WONDERFULLY FRAGRANT AND DELICATE DISH, SIMPLY COMBINE DELICIOUS FRESH SEAFOOD, ROLL THE MIXTURE INTO BALLS AND BAKE THEM IN PAPER PARCELS. AVOID USING SEAFOODS THAT MAY BECOME TOUGH, SUCH AS MUSSELS AND LARGE PIECES OF CALAMARI.

120 G (4¼ OZ) ALL-PURPOSE POTATOES, CUT INTO SMALL CHUNKS
40 G (1½ OZ/¼ CUP) FROZEN BABY PEAS
250 G (9 OZ) MARINARA MIX – PRAWNS (SHRIMP), FISH AND SCALLOPS
250 G (9 OZ) FIRM WHITE FISH FILLET (SUCH AS BARRAMUNDI, SNAPPER, FLATHEAD, WHITING)
3 TABLESPOONS CHOPPED DILL, PLUS EXTRA FOR BAKING
3 TABLESPOONS CHOPPED CHIVES
ZEST OF ½ LEMON
20 CAPERS, ABOUT 6 G (⅛ OZ), RINSED AND DRAINED
¼ FRESH RED CHILLI
1½ TABLESPOONS LEMON-INFUSED OLIVE OIL
1 LEMON, THINLY SLICED
2 GARLIC CLOVES, THINLY SLICED
1 TABLESPOON BUTTER

Place the potato chunks in lightly salted water in a large saucepan over high heat and bring to the boil. Cook for around 10 minutes until the potatoes are cooked all the way through. Drain and set aside to cool.

While the potatoes are cooking, drop the peas in a small saucepan of lightly salted boiling water and cook for 3–4 minutes. Drain and set aside to cool.

In a food processor, gently blitz the seafood, cooled potato, dill, chives, lemon zest, capers, chilli, cooled peas and lemon-infused olive oil, taking care not to overwork the mixture.

Preheat the oven to 120°C (235°F) and add a small ovenproof saucer of water to the back of the oven to create humidity.

Using your hands, gently roll the mixture into 50 g (1¾ oz) balls.

Spread four pieces of baking paper out and lay lemon slices and the extra dill down the middle of each piece. Place three or four balls on each piece of paper, covering the lemon and dill. Add some garlic slices and a small dab of butter on top of each ball. Fold over the long edges of the baking paper, twisting the ends together to seal the seafood balls in the paper. Tie off the ends securely with cooking string. Continue the process with the rest of the mixture until you have about four bags for baking.

Cook in the humid oven for 18 minutes.

Serve immediately.

Sotto palle

Fregola, fresh ricotta & pepitas (p 145) or
Fried pickled zucchini (p 148) or
Italian beans (p 154)

Sauces

Aioli (p 160) or
Green sauce (p 164) or
Seafood bisque (p 165)

Garnishes *(pp 166-9)*

Citrus zest or
Flavoured butter or
Prawn oil

ROAST PUMPKIN, PINE NUTS & CURRANTS

OVEN BAKE

MAKES 30 MEATBALLS

ROASTED PUMPKIN IS FRAGRANT AND SWEET AND MAKES THE PERFECT INGREDIENT IN A MEATBALL. HERE IT'S COMBINED WITH PINE NUTS, CURRANTS AND A VARIETY OF MINCED (GROUND) MEATS.

400 G (14 OZ) PUMPKIN (WINTER SQUASH), CUT INTO SMALL CHUNKS
4 ROSEMARY SPRIGS, LEAVES PICKED AND CHOPPED
10 SAGE LEAVES, CHOPPED
1 TEASPOON FRESHLY GRATED NUTMEG
2 TABLESPOONS PINE NUTS, PLUS EXTRA FOR GARNISH (OPTIONAL)
40 G (1½ OZ/¼ CUP) CURRANTS, PLUS EXTRA FOR GARNISH (OPTIONAL)
2 TEASPOONS MILD PAPRIKA
30 G (1 OZ) BUTTER
OLIVE OIL
90 G (3¼ OZ) DRY BREADCRUMBS
100 G (3½ OZ) MINCED (GROUND) VEAL
100 G (3½ OZ) MINCED (GROUND) PORK
300 G (10½ OZ) MINCED (GROUND) CHICKEN THIGH
60 G (2¼ OZ) PECORINO CHEESE, FINELY GRATED
2 EGGS
OLIVE OIL SPRAY, FOR BAKING

Preheat the oven to 180°C (350°F).

Combine the pumpkin in a baking tray with the rosemary, sage, nutmeg, pine nuts, currants, paprika and butter, and drizzle with lots of olive oil. Season with salt and pepper. Cook in the oven for at least 30 minutes, turning at least once to ensure the pine nuts do not burn.

Remove from the oven and add 30 g (1 oz/¼ cup) breadcrumbs before mashing the pumpkin mix with a fork. Set aside to cool.

Turn the oven up to 200°C (400°F).

Season the veal, pork and chicken with salt and pepper and combine all of the ingredients together (including the cooled pumpkin mix). Using your hands, roll the mixture into 40 g (1½ oz) balls and roll them through the remaining breadcrumbs.

Gently place the balls in a baking tray. Spray the balls with olive oil and bake them in the dry oven for 6–8 minutes.

Serve immediately, with some extra pine nuts and currants sprinkled on top, if desired.

Sotto palle

Couscous with muscatels & pistachios (p 148) or
Fregola, fresh ricotta & pepitas (p 145) or
Roasted pumpkin (p 152)

Sauces

Aioli (p 160) or
Butter & sage sauce (p 159) or
White sauce (p 158)

Garnishes *(pp 166-9)*

Citrus zest or
Toasted pistachios or
Truffle salt

TOFU & MUSHROOM

OVEN BAKE

MAKES *18* VEGIE BALLS

These balls are so flavoursome you won't even know they are missing the meat! When passed through a potato ricer, tofu is an amazing ingredient to use in various styles of vegie balls. Here it's combined with mushrooms, which add an earthy flavour.

20 G (3/4 OZ) PORCINI MUSHROOMS
WARM WATER, FOR SOAKING
90 ML (3 FL OZ) OLIVE OIL
300 G (10½ OZ) PORTOBELLO MUSHROOMS, FINELY DICED
6 SAGE LEAVES, CHOPPED
2 GARLIC CLOVES, FINELY DICED
600 G (1 LB 5 OZ) FIRM TOFU
50 G (1¾ OZ/½ CUP) PECANS, CHOPPED
2 EGGS
60 G (2¼ OZ) MOZZARELLA CHEESE, MELTED (OPTIONAL)
OLIVE OIL SPRAY, FOR BAKING

Soak the dried porcini mushrooms in the warm water until they become soft and rehydrated. Strain, then coarsely chop the porcini mushrooms.

Pour about 2 tablespoons of the olive oil in a frying pan and set over medium heat. Add the portobello mushrooms and sage, and sauté for about 3–4 minutes. Add the softened porcini mushrooms and garlic, and cook for around 6 minutes. Set aside to cool.

Preheat the oven to 180°C (350°F) and add a small ovenproof saucer of water to the back of the oven to create humidity.

Pass the tofu through a potato ricer into a mixing bowl and season with salt and pepper. Add 2½ tablespoons of olive oil, the pecans and egg. If desired, you can add the melted mozzarella cheese. Combine thoroughly and roll the mixture into 50 g (1¾ oz) balls.

Spray a baking tray with olive oil and carefully place the balls in the tray. Bake in the humid oven for 10 minutes.

Serve while hot.

Sotto palle

Grilled mushrooms with taleggio cheese (p 150) or
Simple mushroom risotto (p 149) or
Toasted quinoa, lentils & corn (p 152)

Sauces

Creamy mushroom sauce (p 164)
Green sauce (p 164) or
Sofritto (p 159)

Garnishes *(pp 166-9)*

Pickled zucchini or
Toasted pistachios or
Truffle salt

WINEBAR

CHICKPEA & CAULIFLOWER

MAKES **24** VEGIE BALLS

VEGETARIANS WILL LOVE THESE VEGIE BALLS. THEY CAN BE BAKED IN THE OVEN OR, IF A CRUNCHY EXTERIOR IS PREFERRED, YOU CAN DEEP-FRY THEM. THE CREAMY CAULIFLOWER MAKES THESE BALLS APPEAR VERY DECADENT WHILE REMAINING SUPER LIGHT TO EAT.

- 750 G (1 LB 10 OZ) TINNED CHICKPEAS
- 500 ML (17 FL OZ/2 CUPS) MILK
- 1 LARGE CAULIFLOWER, CUT INTO FLORETS
- 30 G (1 OZ/1 SMALL BUNCH) CORIANDER (CILANTRO), LEAVES PICKED AND CHOPPED
- 2 TEASPOONS GROUND CORIANDER SEEDS
- 2 TEASPOONS GROUND CUMIN SEEDS
- 1 TABLESPOON SUMAC
- 1 ZUCCHINI (COURGETTE), GRATED
- ZEST OF ½ ORANGE
- 50 G (1¾ OZ/½ CUP) FINELY GRATED PARMESAN CHEESE
- OLIVE OIL SPRAY, IF BAKING
- VEGETABLE OIL, IF FRYING

Blitz the majority of the chickpeas in a food processor until smooth. Keep some of the whole chickpeas aside to add some texture inside the balls.

Pour the milk into a large saucepan, add the cauliflower florets and place over medium heat, ensuring the milk doesn't boil. Cook until the cauliflower is soft. Blitz most of the cauliflower and milk in a food processor, keeping aside some of the cauliflower florets to add a different texture to the balls. Once blitzed and cooled, combine all of the ingredients in a mixing bowl and fold everything together using your hands. Season the mixture with salt and pepper.

If baking, preheat the oven to 180°C (350°F).

Gently roll the mixture into 60 g (2¼ oz) balls and carefully place them into half-sphere silicone baking moulds. Alternatively, place the balls into a baking tray sprayed with olive oil. Ensure all the balls are placed neatly together so that they touch the balls next to them. This will help the balls keep their shape. Bake in the dry oven for 8 minutes.

If frying, pour vegetable oil into a large saucepan until it's at least half full and place over medium–high heat until the oil reaches approximately 160–180°C (315–350°F). The oil is ready when breadcrumbs sizzle but do not burn when added to the oil. Once it's the correct temperature, drop in a few balls, one at a time, and cook until golden. This should take around 2–4 minutes. Remove them from the oil and place them on paper towel to absorb any excess oil.

Serve while hot.

Sotto palle

Fried pickled zucchini (p 148) or
Italian beans (p 154) or
Roasted fennel with almond & lemon butter crumb (p 153)

Sauces

Green sauce (p 164) or
Sofritto (p 159) or
White sauce (p 158)

Garnishes *(pp 166-9)*

Cracked black pepper or
Herb oil or
Parmesan crisps

CORN & QUINOA

OVEN BAKE

MAKES **38** VEGIE BALLS

QUINOA IS THE MAIN COMPONENT IN THIS BALL, A WONDERFULLY VERSATILE INGREDIENT THAT CREATES AN INTERESTING TEXTURE FOR THESE VEGETARIAN BALLS. TRY USING IT WITH VARIOUS OTHER INGREDIENTS TO COME UP WITH YOUR OWN VERSION. HERE, WE'VE USED CORN AS THE MAIN FLAVOUR AND HAVE INTRODUCED GRATED VEGETABLES, WHICH HOLD MOISTURE SO THE VEGIE BALLS DON'T BECOME TOO DRY.

250 G (9 OZ/1¼ CUPS) QUINOA
150 G (5½ OZ/¾ CUP) COOKED CORN CUT OFF THE COB, APPROXIMATELY 1½ COBS, CRUSHED WITH A FORK
3 TABLESPOONS ROASTED ALMONDS, CHOPPED
150 G (5½ OZ) FETA CHEESE, CUT INTO ½ CM (¼ IN) CUBES
90 G (3¼ OZ/⅔ CUP) GRATED ZUCCHINI (COURGETTE)
60 G (2¼ OZ) GRATED CARROT
90 ML (3 FL OZ) OLIVE OIL
90 G (3¼ OZ/¾ CUP) DRY BREADCRUMBS
3 EGGS, WHISKED
2 TEASPOONS GROUND NUTMEG
ZEST OF ½ LEMON
OLIVE OIL SPRAY, FOR COATING

Cook the quinoa following the packet directions.

Preheat the oven to 180°C (350°F).

Combine all the ingredients together in a mixing bowl, season with salt and pepper and roll the mixture into 50 g (1¾ oz) balls.

Spray each of the balls with olive oil spray before placing them carefully into a baking tray.

Bake in the dry oven for 10 minutes.

Serve while hot.

Sotto palle

Fried pickled zucchini (p 148) or
Roasted pumpkin (p 152) or
Toasted quinoa, lentils & corn (p 152)

Sauces

Butter & sage sauce (p 159) or
Green sauce (p 164) or
Sofritto (p 159)

Garnishes *(pp 166-9)*

Citrus zest or
Micro herbs or
Salt flakes

I'M A BALLER, BABY!

SOTTO PALLE, SAUCES & GARNISHES

The ultimate meatball experience is all about the balance and contrast of flavours and textures created by the interaction of four separate elements: the meatballs; what accompanies them (sotto palle); what ties it all together (sauces); and what finishes the dish (garnishes). This chapter highlights the accompaniments that will complete your meatball dish. Feel free to adapt these recipes and come up with your own combinations – the beauty of meatballs is that they are incredibly versatile and can go with just about anything.

Sotto Palle

soh - toh - pa - le

In Italian, the word *sotto* means 'beneath' or 'below' and *palle* means 'balls' – which makes the literal translation 'under balls'. Sotto palle is the term we use to describe the component of a dish that complements your meatballs; these delicious foods are what your balls sit on (they could also be called sides). All sotto palle recipes serve four – adjust the recipes accordingly if you wish to create larger or smaller portions. In this chapter you will learn how to make 20 incredibly simple, tasty sotto palle. They all work as stand-alone recipes, but when combined with meatballs and sauce, they create the ultimate meatball experience.

Sauces

The one thing that makes your meatballs and sotto palle sing in harmony is sauce. Never underestimate the difference a good sauce makes to a meatball dish. Sauces not only bring moisture and flavour to your dish, they can complement and unite all the elements on your plate, bringing your entire meatball-eating experience to a whole new level. In this section, we present 20 sauces that have been designed specifically to accompany your meatballs and sotto palle.

Garnishes

A simple garnish can seem such a trivial thing, but it can elevate any meatball dish. A garnish can be used to add texture or freshness, introduce another layer of complexity or simply make a striking visual impression. Many of these garnishes can be made ahead of time and stored in the refrigerator for use across multiple recipes.

COLOSSUS
OIL
EPSON

CREAMY (OR GRILLED) POLENTA

SERVES 4

WARM POLENTA WILL GO WITH ALMOST ANY STYLE OF MEATBALL. THIS RECIPE USES CHICKEN STOCK BUT YOU CAN EASILY SUBSTITUTE IT WITH VEGETABLE STOCK TO MAKE IT VEGETARIAN.

- 800 ML (28 FL OZ) MILK
- 200 ML (7 FL OZ) CHICKEN STOCK
- 240 G (8½ OZ) POLENTA (CORNMEAL)
- 80 G (2¾ OZ/¾ CUP) FINELY GRATED PARMESAN CHEESE
- 100 G (3½ OZ) BUTTER, CUT INTO CUBES
- TRUFFLE OIL (OPTIONAL)
- PINCH OF GROUND NUTMEG, TO TASTE (OPTIONAL)

Warm the milk and chicken stock in a deep saucepan over medium heat. Just before boiling point, add 1 teaspoon of salt and the polenta, stirring continuously with a whisk. Keep whisking until the polenta is cooked (it's ready when it's no longer grainy). This process should take 45 minutes.

Remove the saucepan from the heat and stir through the parmesan and butter. The final consistency should be thick and creamy. Add a drizzle of truffle oil and a sprinkling of nutmeg if you want.

To make grilled polenta, add 100 g (3½ oz) extra polenta to the hot milky stock and whisk until fully cooked. Spread the polenta out on a tray and put in the fridge until firm. Cut the polenta into any shape you'd like, dust with a little more polenta, then fry in a hot pan with some olive oil until golden.

BUTTERED RISONI & PEAS

SERVES 4

RISONI IS A TYPE OF PASTA THAT COOKS QUICKLY AND LOOKS A LOT LIKE RICE. IT'S READILY AVAILABLE AT MOST GROCERY STORES. RISONI CAN BE MADE AHEAD OF TIME AND BROUGHT TO TEMPERATURE IN A PAN WITH SOME GOOD-QUALITY BUTTER. DELICIOUS SWEET PEAS PERFECTLY COMPLEMENT THIS COMFORTING SOTTO PALLE DISH.

- 300 G (10½ OZ) RISONI
- 200 G (7 OZ/1½ CUPS) FROZEN PEAS
- 20 G (¾ OZ) BUTTER
- 12 SAGE LEAVES, COARSELY CHOPPED

Cook the risoni in a saucepan of salted boiling water over medium heat for around 8 minutes to the point where it is still slightly *al dente*. Add the peas to the pan to cook with the risoni in the last couple of minutes.

Once cooked and strained, add the risoni and peas back into the pan, add the butter and stir through. Add the sage and season to taste with salt and pepper.

SUPER POTATO SMASH

SERVES 4

THIS MIGHT JUST BE THE HERO OF ALL MEATBALL SOTTO PALLE! FOR THIS DISH, LEAVE THE SKINS ON YOUR POTATOES — IT RESULTS IN A MORE RUSTIC AND TEXTURED DISH. SPS IS UNBEATABLE AS IT WORKS WELL WITH VIRTUALLY ALL MEATBALLS AND ALL SAUCES.

1 KG (2 LB 4 OZ) NEW POTATOES
200 ML (7 FL OZ) CREAM
200 G (7 OZ) BUTTER, CUT INTO CUBES
30 G (1 OZ/1 SMALL BUNCH) FLAT-LEAF (ITALIAN) PARSLEY, LEAVES PICKED AND CHOPPED

Put the potatoes in a large saucepan of lightly salted water over high heat and bring to the boil. Reduce the heat and cook for about 15–20 minutes until they are soft.

Once the potatoes are cooked, strain the water from the pot and use a potato masher to begin to smash the potatoes. Once partially smashed, add the cream and butter and stir. Season with salt and pepper and finally stir through the parsley for freshness.

FREGOLA, FRESH RICOTTA & PEPITAS

SERVES 4

FREGOLA IS A TYPE OF PASTA THAT RESEMBLES COUSCOUS. WHEN COOKED, IT SWELLS INTO LOVELY MORSELS, WHICH ARE PERFECT TO REST YOUR MEATBALLS ON. THE RICOTTA SMOOTHES OUT THIS DISH, WHILE THE PEPITAS ADD SOME CRUNCH.

350 G (12 OZ) FREGOLA
50 G (1¾ OZ) PEPITAS (PUMPKIN SEEDS)
2½ TABLESPOONS OLIVE OIL
200 G (7 OZ) FRESH RICOTTA CHEESE
10 G (¼ OZ/½ BUNCH) TARRAGON LEAVES, ROUGHLY TORN
JUICE OF ½ SMALL LEMON

Cook the fregola in a saucepan of salted water, following the packet directions, until done.

Toast the pepitas in a dry frying pan over medium heat for around 3 minutes until they start to take on some colour.

Strain the pasta and combine in a mixing bowl with the olive oil, ricotta cheese, tarragon and pepitas. Add the lemon juice and season to taste, stirring everything through.

You can enjoy this dish either warm or cold.

LASAGNE SHEETS

SERVES 4

Meatballs and pasta – it's as if they were made for each other. Here is a basic pasta dough recipe, which will form the base of your lasagne sheets. Simply roll out the pasta into thin sheets and cut them into portions that are about the length of a plate. The cooked pasta sheets can be layered over the plate, creating the ultimate bed for your meatballs.

200 G (7 OZ/1⅓ CUPS) 00 FLOUR
2 EGGS, GENTLY WHISKED
3 TABLESPOONS EXTRA VIRGIN OLIVE OIL
50 G (1¾ OZ) BUTTER

On your work surface, sift the flour and a pinch of salt into a mound and create a well in the centre. Pour the egg and 1 tablespoon of the olive oil into the well and start to incorporate them into the flour with your fingers. Knead for around 10 minutes until the dough is pliable. If too wet, add more flour; if too dry, add more olive oil or some water.

Form a ball with the dough, then wrap it in plastic wrap and place in the refrigerator to rest for 30 minutes.

To form the lasagna, use a pasta machine to roll the dough out into flat sheets. Make sure they don't become too thin, or they'll break apart too easily. It's also easy to use a rolling pin and roll out the pasta by hand.

Once the pasta sheets are ready, cut them into segments, around 10–15 cm (4–6 in) long.

In a large saucepan, bring water to the boil and add a good pinch of salt. Drop in the pasta segments a few at a time. Once they rise to the top, the pasta is ready. This should only take 1–2 minutes. Drain the pasta sheets, but retain a little of the cooking water.

In a large mixing bowl, combine the butter, 2 tablespoons of olive oil and some salt with around 3 tablespoons of the hot cooking water to melt the butter. Now transfer the cooked pasta to the mixing bowl and toss the pasta around to coat each of the pasta sheets.

Remove from the mixing bowl and place 2–3 sheets of pasta on each warm plate, ready for the meatballs to go over the top.

PEA, MINT & RICOTTA SALAD

SERVES 4

THIS SIMPLE, FRESH DISH IS PERFECT TO ACCOMPANY ANY OF YOUR MEATBALLS. THIS WORKS PARTICULARLY WELL WITH ANY CHICKEN-BASED MEATBALL. YOU CAN SUBSTITUTE THE AIR-DRIED RICOTTA FOR ANY STYLE OF YOUR PREFERRED CHEESE.

500 G (1 LB 2 OZ/3¼ CUPS) FRESH, SHELLED PEAS (YOU CAN ALSO USE FROZEN)
10 MINT LEAVES, TORN
100 G (3½ OZ) DRIED RICOTTA CHEESE, CRUMBLED
120 G (4¼ OZ) MIXED LETTUCE LEAVES – RADICCHIO, COS (ROMAINE), LAMB'S LETTUCE (CORN SALAD)

VINAIGRETTE

15 ML (½ FL OZ) CHARDONNAY VINEGAR (OR GOOD-QUALITY WHITE WINE VINEGAR)
JUICE OF ½ LEMON
80 ML (2½ FL OZ/⅓ CUP) EXTRA VIRGIN OLIVE OIL

Blanch the peas in boiling salted water for about 4 minutes, then refresh in an ice bath. Strain the peas.

To make the vinaigrette, whisk the vinegar, lemon juice and olive oil thoroughly in a small bowl. Season with salt and pepper.

Add all the ingredients into a serving dish and toss.

BUTTERED EDAMAME

SERVES 4

EDAMAME ARE OFTEN SERVED AS A STARTER ON JAPANESE MENUS. THEIR FIRM TEXTURE IS A WONDERFUL CONTRAST TO SOFT MEATBALLS, WHICH IS WHY THEY MAKE A FANTASTIC SOTTO PALLE. IF YOU ARE UNABLE TO FIND FRESH EDAMAME, FROZEN EDAMAME ARE PERFECTLY FINE AND ARE READILY AVAILABLE FROM MOST ASIAN GROCERY STORES.

500 G (1 LB 2 OZ) EDAMAME (GREEN SOYA BEANS)
20 G (¾ OZ) BUTTER
ZEST OF 1 ORANGE
1 TEASPOON SESAME OIL

Boil the edamame in lightly salted water in a saucepan over medium heat for around 3 minutes, and then drain.

Melt the butter in a saucepan over low heat. Once it starts to bubble, add the drained edamame and toss. Season with a little salt and orange zest, and stir through the sesame oil.

FRIED PICKLED ZUCCHINI

SERVES 4

UNTIL YOU TRY THIS DISH YOU WON'T BELIEVE SOMETHING SO SIMPLE CAN TASTE SO GOOD. IT'S AN OLD-SCHOOL RECIPE THAT OFTEN APPEARS ON AN ANTIPASTO PLATE ON AN ITALIAN TABLE.

3 ZUCCHINI (COURGETTES)
VEGETABLE OIL, FOR FRYING
150 ML (5 FL OZ) APPLE CIDER VINEGAR
EXTRA VIRGIN OLIVE OIL (OPTIONAL)

Use a mandoline to finely slice the zucchini into 2 mm (1/16 cm) slices.

Pour vegetable oil into a frying pan until it's a quarter full and set it over high heat. Once the oil is hot, fry the zucchini slices in batches for around 30 seconds on each side. Drain each batch on paper towel before placing them on the serving dish. Repeat until all the zucchini slices are cooked.

Remove most of the excess oil from the pan, then add the apple cider vinegar and bring to the boil. Take off the heat and pour the vinegar over the zucchini (you won't need to use all the vinegar – only enough to wet all of the zucchini slices).

Season with salt and pepper to taste and serve hot or cold, with a drizzle of extra virgin olive oil if desired.

COUSCOUS WITH MUSCATELS & PISTACHIOS

SERVES 4

THIS DISH CAN BE ENJOYED HOT OR COLD. COUSCOUS IS A GREAT RETAINER FOR SAUCE, WHICH IS WHY THIS DISH WORKS SO WELL AS A SOTTO PALLE. THE MUSCATELS ADD SWEETNESS AND THE PISTACHIOS ARE AWESOME (JUST BECAUSE).

350 ML (12 FL OZ) VEGETABLE STOCK
250 G (9 OZ/1⅓ CUPS) COUSCOUS
1¼ TABLESPOONS OLIVE OIL
50 G (1¾ OZ/⅓ CUP) PISTACHIO NUT KERNELS
75 G (2½ OZ) MUSCATELS
15 G (½ OZ/½ SMALL BUNCH) CORIANDER (CILANTRO), LEAVES PICKED AND FINELY CHOPPED
1 TEASPOON SALT FLAKES
1 TABLESPOON LEMON JUICE

Bring the stock to the boil in a saucepan and then stir in the couscous. Cover with a lid, remove the pan from the heat and allow the couscous to absorb the stock for 10 minutes.

Transfer the couscous to the serving dish. Add the olive oil and gently fluff the couscous with a fork. Add the pistachios, muscatels, coriander, salt flakes and lemon juice, and mix through.

SIMPLE MUSHROOM RISOTTO

SERVES 4

RISOTTO IS THE KING OF ALL RICE DISHES. ONCE MASTERED, RISOTTO CAN FORM THE BASE OF ANY MEATBALL FEAST, OR CAN STAND ALONE AS THE HERO OF THE DISH. TAKE YOUR TIME WITH RISOTTO AND USE THE VERY FINEST INGREDIENTS YOU CAN GET YOUR HANDS ON – YOU WON'T BE DISAPPOINTED.

- 40 G (1½ OZ) DRIED PORCINI MUSHROOMS
- WARM WATER, FOR SOAKING
- 1.75 LITRES (61 FL OZ/7 CUPS) STOCK (CHICKEN OR VEGETABLE)
- 100 G (3½ OZ) BUTTER
- OLIVE OIL
- ½ BROWN ONION, FINELY DICED
- 1 SMALL LEEK, PALE PART ONLY, FINELY DICED
- 3 GARLIC CLOVES, FINELY DICED
- 12 FRESH SAGE LEAVES, COARSELY CHOPPED
- SALT FLAKES
- 150 G (5½ OZ) PORTOBELLO MUSHROOMS (OR FRESH PORCINI IF AVAILABLE), SLICED
- 440 G (15½ OZ/2 CUPS) ARBORIO RICE
- 150 ML (5 FL OZ) WHITE WINE
- 30 G (1 OZ/1 SMALL BUNCH) FLAT-LEAF (ITALIAN) PARSLEY, LEAVES PICKED AND CHOPPED
- ZEST OF ½ ORANGE
- 100 G (3½ OZ/1 CUP) FINELY GRATED PARMESAN CHEESE
- TRUFFLE SALT (OPTIONAL)

Rehydrate the porcini mushrooms in the warm water. Once the mushrooms are soft, strain the residual liquid through gauze and add the liquid to a large saucepan with the stock over low–medium heat. Bring the stock up to a gentle simmer.

Meanwhile, in a heavy-set saucepan over low–medium heat, melt half the butter with a good drizzle of olive oil. Add the onion and leek and cook for about 3–4 minutes. Add the garlic and half of the sage. Season with salt flakes. Add the portobello mushrooms and sauté everything for a few minutes.

Gradually turn up the temperature and add the rice to the pan, stirring with a wooden spoon to coat all the rice granules until they become glossy. Add the white wine. Once the rice has absorbed the white wine, start adding a ladle of stock at a time, continuously stirring. Add the porcini mushrooms. Continue to add the stock, stirring until each ladle of stock is absorbed and the rice is cooked to your liking. Slightly *al dente* is preferred.

Turn off the heat and rapidly stir through the rest of the butter, then add the remainder of the sage, parsley, orange zest, a good hit of cracked black pepper and then the parmesan cheese. Stir briefly, then cover the pot with a lid and let it sit for 10 minutes before serving. Season with truffle salt if you so desire.

Note: If you don't have gauze available to strain the mushrooms, you can use a clean kitchen tea towel (dish towel) instead.

PANZANELLA

SERVES 4

HEIRLOOM TOMATOES OF DIFFERENT COLOURS MAKE THIS VERSION OF A TIMELESS PANZANELLA REALLY STAND OUT. TOASTED CROUTONS DOUSED IN WHITE BALSAMIC VINEGAR GIVE THE DISH AN INCREDIBLE CRUNCH, AND THE TORN BASIL WILL TRANSPORT YOU INTO THE HEART OF TUSCANY.

½ DAY-OLD BAGUETTE
EXTRA VIRGIN OLIVE OIL, FOR DRIZZLING
10–15 (DEPENDING ON SIZE) VINE-RIPENED OR HEIRLOOM TOMATOES
15 BASIL LEAVES, TORN
SALT FLAKES
WHITE BALSAMIC VINEGAR, FOR DRIZZLING

Preheat the oven to 120°C (235°F).

Cut the crusts off the bread. Take the soft inner bread and cut into bite-sized pieces. Drizzle with olive oil and toast lightly in the oven for about 10 minutes.

Slice the tomatoes into quarters. Drizzle with olive oil, add the basil leaves and season with salt flakes and freshly ground pepper to taste. Just before serving, drizzle white balsamic vinegar over the toasted bread and add it to the salad. Serve immediately.

GRILLED MUSHROOMS WITH TALEGGIO CHEESE

SERVES 4

THERE'S NOTHING QUITE LIKE PERFECTLY GRILLED MUSHROOMS, EXCEPT WHEN THEY ARE COVERED IN MELTED ITALIAN TALEGGIO CHEESE. YOU AND YOUR MEATBALLS ARE SURE TO BE IN HEAVEN.

12 LARGE PORTOBELLO MUSHROOMS
OLIVE OIL, FOR DRIZZLING
2 GARLIC CLOVES, FINELY DICED
50 G (1¾ OZ) BUTTER
120 G (4¼ OZ) TALEGGIO CHEESE

Preheat the oven to 180°C (350°F).

Skin the mushrooms and remove the stems. Cut a few crosses on the inside of the mushroom to help with even cooking. Season with salt and pepper, and lightly drizzle with olive oil. Bake in the oven for 15 minutes.

While the mushrooms are cooking, make the garlic butter by gently combining the garlic and the butter. Season with salt and pepper.

When the mushrooms are cooked and have cooled down, smear the inside with the garlic butter and add about 10 g (1/4 oz) of taleggio cheese per mushroom. Place them back in the oven for 5 minutes until the butter and cheese have melted.

BASIC PEPERONATA

SERVES 4

THIS BASIC PEPERONATA RELIES ON THE DEEP FLAVOURS OF CAPSICUM AND EGGPLANT TO CARRY THE DISH. CONVENIENTLY IT CAN BE MADE AHEAD OF TIME AND KEPT IN THE REFRIGERATOR FOR LATER USE. IT ALSO DOUBLES AS AN AMAZING PASTA SAUCE IF YOU BLEND IT WITH SOME EXTRA OLIVE OIL.

- 4 RED OR YELLOW CAPSICUMS (PEPPERS), OR A COMBINATION OF BOTH
- 3 TABLESPOONS OLIVE OIL
- ½ EGGPLANT (AUBERGINE), CUT INTO 1 CM (½ IN) CUBES
- 1 LARGE ZUCCHINI (COURGETTE), CUT INTO 1 CM (½ IN) CUBES
- 1 DRIED BAY LEAF
- 6 BASIL LEAVES, TORN
- 15 G (½ OZ/½ SMALL BUNCH) FLAT-LEAF (ITALIAN) PARSLEY, LEAVES PICKED AND CHOPPED
- 1 FRESH RED CHILLI, FINELY SLICED (OPTIONAL EXTRA)

Preheat the oven grill (broiler). Set to high.

Place the capsicums under a very hot grill until the skin starts to bubble and turn black. You may have to turn the capsicums regularly for the skin to be exposed on all sides. Once all of the capsicums have scorched, remove them from the grill. This should take about 10–15 minutes. Place them inside a plastic bag and tie it off. This will steam the capsicums without overcooking them.

After 15–30 minutes, open the bag and remove the capsicums. Remove the skin and clean the inside of the capsicums, making sure to retain all of the juices. Slice the capsicums into strips and set aside.

Heat up the olive oil in a frying pan over medium heat and add the eggplant, zucchini and bay leaf. Cook for around 5 minutes, then add the capsicum strips and all their juices. Continue to cook for a further 5 minutes and season with salt and pepper. Remove the bay leaf, add the basil and parsley, and stir through. If you're after heat, sliced red chilli works a treat.

WASABI SLAW

SERVES 4

NOT DISSIMILAR TO A TRADITIONAL MAYONNAISE COLESLAW, THIS DELICIOUS SOTTO PALLE USES WASABI FOR EXTRA KICK, WHICH MAKES THIS DISH PERFECT FOR ANY RICH MEATBALLS, ESPECIALLY PORK.

- 400 G (14 OZ) RED AND GREEN CABBAGE, THINLY SLICED
- 3 GRANNY SMITH APPLES, SLICED AND JULIENNED
- 30 G (1 OZ/1 SMALL BUNCH) FLAT-LEAF (ITALIAN) PARSLEY, LEAVES PICKED AND CHOPPED
- 150 G (5½ OZ) AIOLI, WITH OPTIONAL WASABI (P 160)
- 100 G (3½ OZ) FENNEL, SLICED
- 150 G (5½ OZ) CARROT, GRATED

Combine all ingredients in a mixing bowl, season with salt and pepper to taste, and mix thoroughly.

ROASTED PUMPKIN

SERVES 4

A SUPER EASY ONE-POT WONDER, THIS FLAVOUR-PACKED PUMPKIN DISH IS THE PERFECT ACCOMPANIMENT TO MOST MEATBALL RECIPES.

- 1 KG (2 LB 4 OZ) PUMPKIN (WINTER SQUASH), CUT INTO CHUNKS
- 6 ROSEMARY SPRIGS, LEAVES PICKED AND CHOPPED
- 12 SAGE LEAVES, CHOPPED
- 1 TEASPOON FRESHLY GRATED NUTMEG
- 50 G (1¾ OZ/⅓ CUP) PINE NUTS
- 50 G (1¾ OZ/⅓ CUP) CURRANTS
- 1 TEASPOON MILD PAPRIKA
- 30 G (1 OZ) BUTTER
- 3 TABLESPOONS OLIVE OIL
- 60 G (2¼ OZ) PECORINO CHEESE
- 30 G (1 OZ/1 SMALL BUNCH) FLAT-LEAF (ITALIAN) PARSLEY, LEAVES PICKED AND CHOPPED

Preheat the oven to 180°C (350°F).

On a baking tray, combine the pumpkin with the rosemary, sage, nutmeg, pine nuts, currants, paprika, butter, salt and pepper. Drizzle with the olive oil. Cook in the oven for at least 30 minutes, turning the pumpkin over at least once during the cooking process and ensuring the pine nuts do not burn.

Remove from the oven and finely grate the pecorino cheese over the top, then sprinkle with chopped parsley for freshness.

TOASTED QUINOA, LENTILS & CORN

SERVES 4

QUINOA IS A PERFECT BASE FOR ANY STYLE OF MEATBALL. HERE WE'VE TOASTED THE COOKED QUINOA IN A HOT PAN WITH BUTTER TO MAKE IT NUTTIER AND MORE FLAVOURSOME. ADD YOUR FAVOURITE VEGETABLES (ZUCCHINI, PEAS, CARROTS, WHATEVER YOU FEEL LIKE ON THE DAY) TO MAKE THIS SOTTO PALLE YOUR OWN.

- 100 G (3½ OZ/½ CUP) QUINOA, RINSED
- 50 G (1¾ OZ) BUTTER
- EXTRA VIRGIN OLIVE OIL
- 200 G (7 OZ/1 CUP) COOKED CORN CUT OFF THE COB, APPROXIMATELY 2 COBS
- 100 G (3½ OZ) TINNED LENTILS
- 50 G (1¾ OZ/1 BUNCH) MINT, LEAVES PICKED AND CHOPPED

Cook the quinoa by pouring it into 500 ml (17 fl oz/2 cups) of water in a saucepan over medium–high heat. Bring the water and quinoa to the boil, then reduce the heat to a gentle simmer with the lid on for 25 minutes.

Heat the butter and a good drizzle of olive oil in a deep frying pan over medium heat until it starts to foam, then add the cooked quinoa. Cook for 10 minutes over high heat while constantly stirring so the quinoa doesn't stick to the pan. The quinoa will start to darken slightly and take on a lightly toasted flavour. Add the corn and lentils and continue to cook over high heat for a further 5 minutes.

Take off the heat, add the chopped mint and a good drizzle of olive oil, and season with salt and pepper.

Serve while hot.

ROASTED FENNEL WITH ALMOND & LEMON BUTTER CRUMB

SERVES 4

ROASTED FENNEL TAKES ON A BEAUTIFULLY SWEET YET ROBUST FLAVOUR, WHICH WORKS PERFECTLY AS A SOTTO PALLE FOR MEATBALLS. HERE WE'VE ADDED AN ALMOND AND LEMON CRUMB, AND FINISHED THE DISH IN THE OVEN TO BRING OUT EVEN MORE SWEETNESS FROM THE FENNEL.

- 55 G (2 OZ/⅓ CUP) ALMONDS
- 55 G (2 OZ/½ CUP) DRY BREADCRUMBS
- ZEST OF 1 SMALL LEMON, EXTRA TO FINISH
- 1 GARLIC CLOVE
- 2 FENNEL BULBS, FRONDS RESERVED
- 30 G (1 OZ/⅓ CUP) FINELY GRATED PARMESAN CHEESE, EXTRA TO FINISH
- 30 G (1 OZ/1 SMALL BUNCH) FLAT-LEAF (ITALIAN) PARSLEY, LEAVES PICKED AND COARSELY CHOPPED
- 60 G (2¼ OZ) BUTTER
- 3 FENNEL BULBS
- 2½ TABLESPOONS OLIVE OIL
- FRESHLY GRATED NUTMEG, TO FINISH (OPTIONAL)

To make the crumb, add the almonds, breadcrumbs, lemon zest, garlic, fennel fronds, parmesan cheese, parsley, butter and some salt and pepper, and blitz in a food processor.

Preheat the oven to 160°C (315°F).

Remove the tough outer layer of the fennel bulbs. Cut the fennel into thick slices. Heat up the olive oil in an ovenproof frying pan. Once hot, add the fennel slices and cook over high heat for around 6 minutes, turning the fennel regularly so that all sides take on some colour.

Evenly spread the crumb mixture on top of the fennel and place the pan in the preheated oven for 20 minutes. Once out of the oven, finish by grating some extra parmesan cheese and lemon zest over the top. Some grated nutmeg also works perfectly with this dish.

CHEESY BREAD

SERVES 4

GRILLED BREAD, MELTED CHEESE, TASTY MEATBALLS — NEED WE SAY MORE? MANY A MEATBALL DREAM HAS BEEN FORMED ON A BED OF GRILLED BREAD AND MELTED CHEESE. USE ANY STYLE OF BREAD AND CHEESE YOU LIKE. YOU CAN'T GO WRONG.

- 1 CIABATTA LOAF OR BAGUETTE
- 1 GARLIC CLOVE
- FAVOURITE MELTING CHEESE
- FAVOURITE BUTTER (OPTIONAL)

Preheat the oven grill (broiler). Set to medium.

Cut the bread into thick slices and rub the garlic clove into the bread. It helps to bruise the garlic first. Add slices of cheese to the bread and toast under the grill until bubbling.

Optional: Spread some of your favourite butter over the bread before putting on the cheese.

MINESTRONE

SERVES 4

MINESTRONE CAN BE WHATEVER YOU WANT IT TO BE, AND IT'S THE PERFECT WAY TO USE UP PIECES OF VEGETABLES LEFT OVER FROM THE GARDEN OR REFRIGERATOR. IT'S SIMPLY A CASE OF CHOPPING THEM UP INTO NICE SMALL PIECES AND COOKING THEM IN A FRAGRANT BROTH.

- 2 CARROTS
- 2 ALL-PURPOSE POTATOES
- 100 G (3½ OZ) PUMPKIN (WINTER SQUASH)
- 2 TOMATOES
- 2 CELERY STALKS
- 2.5 LITRES (87 FL OZ/10 CUPS) STOCK (CHICKEN OR VEGETABLE)
- 100 G (3½ OZ/⅔ CUP) FRESH, SHELLED BABY PEAS (OR ¾ CUP FROZEN BABY PEAS)
- 30 G (1 OZ/1 SMALL BUNCH) FLAT-LEAF (ITALIAN) PARSLEY, LEAVES PICKED AND CHOPPED
- 1 GARLIC CLOVE, THINLY SLICED
- EXTRA VIRGIN OLIVE OIL, TO FINISH
- PARMESAN CHEESE (OPTIONAL)

Chop the carrot, potato, pumpkin, tomato and celery into small pieces – the aim is to be able to get all of the different vegetables onto your spoon at the same time.

Heat up the stock in a large saucepan over medium heat. Add all of the vegetables (including the peas) and cook until the vegetables are just barely cooked through. This should only take around 15 minutes. Stir in the parsley and garlic. Season to taste.

Once served, drizzle some high-quality extra virgin olive oil into each dish. For an extra creamy texture, finely grate some parmesan cheese over the top.

ITALIAN BEANS

SERVES 4

SIMPLE AND ELEGANT, THIS DELICIOUS SOTTO PALLE COMBINES CANNELLINI BEANS WITH HIGH-QUALITY EXTRA VIRGIN OLIVE OIL TO CREATE THE PERFECT ACCOMPANIMENT TO MOST MEATBALL RECIPES. THE TEXTURE OF THIS DISH CAN BE MODIFIED BY COOKING SOME OF THE BEANS MORE THAN OTHERS – SOME WILL BE FIRM TO THE BITE AND OTHERS WILL BE SOFT.

- 450 G (1 LB) DRIED CANNELLINI BEANS
- 25 G (1 OZ/½ BUNCH) FLAT-LEAF (ITALIAN) PARSLEY, LEAVES PICKED AND CHOPPED
- 1 CELERY HEART, DICED
- ZEST OF 1 LEMON
- 2½ TABLESPOONS EXTRA VIRGIN OLIVE OIL

Soak the dried beans in a large bowl or pot of cold water overnight (or for a minimum of 5 hours). Drain and rinse.

Put the beans in a stockpot and fill with water so the beans are completely covered, with at least 5 cm (2 in) of water on top. Bring to the boil over high heat, then boil for a further 10 minutes, intermittently scooping off any foam. Add a little bit of salt and reduce the heat to low, simmering for a further 25 minutes, or until the beans are tender.

Drain the beans and season with salt and pepper, add the parsley, celery, lemon zest and extra virgin olive oil. Mix and serve.

MEATBALL
&
WINE BAR

GORGONZOLA CHEESE SAUCE

MAKES
650 GRAMS (1 LB 7 OZ)

A CLASSIC BLUE CHEESE SAUCE IS HARD TO BEAT! WHEN PAIRED WITH MOST MEATBALL AND SOTTE PALLE COMBOS, THIS DELICIOUS SAUCE CAN CREATE A HIGHLY MEMORABLE FEAST. GORGONZOLA CHEESE COULD OVERPOWER DELICATE INGREDIENTS, SO ADJUST THE QUANTITY TO SUIT.

500 ML (17 FL OZ/2 CUPS) THICK (DOUBLE) CREAM
20 G (¾ OZ) BUTTER
120 G (4¼ OZ) CRUMBLY GORGONZOLA CHEESE
2 TABLESPOONS FINELY GRATED PARMESAN CHEESE
1 HANDFUL WALNUTS (OR PECANS), CHOPPED
ZEST OF ¼ ORANGE
15 G (¾ OZ/½ SMALL BUNCH) FLAT-LEAF (ITALIAN) PARSLEY, LEAVES PICKED AND CHOPPED

Bring the cream and butter to a gentle bubble in a saucepan over medium heat, then lower the heat.

Add the gorgonzola cheese a little at a time, whisking it into the cream until it's all combined. Now incorporate the parmesan cheese. Add the walnuts and orange zest, and season to taste. Finish by mixing in a good whack of freshly chopped parsley.

ITALIAN VEAL JUS

MAKES
800 GRAMS (1 LB 12 OZ)

HERE'S A CLASSIC ITALIAN SAUCE, WHICH USES HIGH-QUALITY VEAL STOCK COMBINED WITH VEGETABLES AND HERBS. TAKE YOUR TIME MAKING THIS SAUCE AND LET IT GENTLY REDUCE TO DEVELOP FLAVOUR.

250 G (9 OZ) DRIED PORCINI MUSHROOMS
WARM WATER, FOR SOAKING
OLIVE OIL
1 ONION, FINELY DICED
1 GARLIC CLOVE, FINELY DICED
1 CELERY STALK, FINELY DICED
100 G (3½ OZ) TOMATO PASTE (CONCENTRATED PURÉE)
200 ML (7 FL OZ) WHITE WINE
200 ML (7 FL OZ) VEAL STOCK
ZEST OF 1 LEMON
2 TABLESPOONS FRESHLY CHOPPED FLAT-LEAF (ITALIAN) PARSLEY
1 THYME SPRIG, LEAVES PICKED AND FINELY CHOPPED

Soak the dried porcini mushrooms in the warm water until they become soft and rehydrated. Slice the porcini mushrooms and set aside.

Heat a good drizzle of olive oil in a heavy-based saucepan over medium heat and start cooking the onion and garlic. Add the celery and cook for several minutes until golden. Add the mushrooms, stir in the tomato paste and cook for a few more minutes. Add the white wine and reduce for a minute or two.

Add the veal stock and the lemon zest, and simmer gently for at least 30 minutes. Finish by adding the parsley and thyme and season with salt and pepper. Continue to simmer for another 3–5 minutes.

LABNA

MAKES
400 GRAMS (14 OZ)

LABNA IS A YOGHURT-BASED SAUCE, WHICH CAN BE TAILOR-MADE TO YOUR TASTE WITH ANY COMBINATION OF HERBS. THE YOGHURT NEEDS TO BE THICKENED AND THIS IS ACHIEVED BY DRAINING IT OVER SEVERAL HOURS.

500 ML (17 FL OZ/2 CUPS) LEBANESE OR GREEK YOGHURT
DILL OR MINT, FRESHLY CHOPPED
EXTRA VIRGIN OLIVE OIL

Moisten two pieces of clean muslin and then wring them out. Line a colander (preferably one with a high base) with two layers of the muslin, ensuring it overhangs the rim of the colander, then place the colander on top of a bowl so the colander base is well above any liquid that drains out.

Add a ½ teaspoon of salt to the yoghurt and combine, then pour the yoghurt over the lined colander and set aside in the refrigerator for at least 6 hours. This will remove the whey from the yoghurt, resulting in a thicker and creamier product.

Once drained, transfer the yoghurt to a bowl and add some freshly chopped herbs and a good drizzle of extra virgin olive oil.

When serving, add some pepper to taste.

CHUNKY ITALIAN RED SAUCE

MAKES
1.4 KILOGRAMS (3 LB 2 OZ)

YOU CAN USE ANY VARIETY OF FRESH TOMATO – FEEL FREE TO LEAVE THE SKINS ON AS THIS ALL ADDS TO THE TEXTURE OF THE SAUCE. THIS WARMING SAUCE CAN BE MADE IN BULK AND USED ACROSS A VARIETY OF DISHES.

OLIVE OIL
1 KG (2 LB 4 OZ) FRESH TOMATOES, DICED
½ BROWN ONION, SLICED
2 GARLIC CLOVES, DICED
1 TABLESPOON TOMATO PASTE (CONCENTRATED PURÉE)
800 G (1 LB 12 OZ) TINNED CHOPPED TOMATOES
50 G (1¾ OZ/1 LARGE BUNCH) BASIL, LEAVES PICKED AND TORN

Start by heating up a drizzle of olive oil in a frying pan over high heat until it starts to smoke. Add the fresh tomato and stir around the pan until they take on some colour and begin to break down. You need to get the pan very hot so that the natural sugars in the tomato come out the moment they make contact with the hot oil.

Add the onion and a pinch of salt. Cook while stirring for 3 minutes, then add the garlic and tomato paste. Once the onion has been partially cooked, add the tinned tomato, reduce the heat to low and cook for at least 1 hour or until reduced by around half.

Season with salt and lots of pepper, and add the torn basil leaves at the end. Finish with another good drizzle of olive oil.

WHITE SAUCE

MAKES
1 KILOGRAM (2 LB 4 OZ)

ONCE YOU'VE TRIED THIS SIMPLE WHITE SAUCE OUT A FEW TIMES, CONSIDER ADDING YOUR FAVOURITE CHEESES OR SPICES TO MAKE IT YOUR OWN. IT'S A TERRIFIC ACCOMPANIMENT TO VEAL AND PORK MEATBALLS.

100 G (3½ OZ) BUTTER
100 G (3½ OZ/⅔ CUP) PLAIN (ALL-PURPOSE) FLOUR
600 ML (21 FL OZ) MILK
200 ML (7 FL OZ) VEGETABLE STOCK
1 DRIED BAY LEAF
60 G (2¼ OZ) FONTINA CHEESE, GRATED

In a saucepan, cook a roux by bringing the butter to a gentle foam over medium heat, then adding the flour and whisking it in to create a paste. Continue to stir until all of the flour has cooked out – this should only take 2–4 minutes.

In a separate saucepan over low heat, heat up the milk and stock with the bay leaf until it just starts to simmer. Remove the bay leaf and slowly add the milky stock to the roux, whisking out any lumps. Continue to cook over low heat while whisking until all the liquid has been absorbed. Remove from the heat. Add the Fontina cheese and season to taste.

ROASTED CAPSICUM SAUCE

MAKES
400 GRAMS (14 OZ)

ROASTED CAPSICUM BECOMES SWEET AND TENDER WHEN COOKED AT HIGH HEAT IN THE OVEN AND MAKES A WONDERFUL ACCOMPANIMENT TO MEATBALLS, PARTICULARLY WHEN PROCESSED TO A SMOOTH CONSISTENCY.

4 RED CAPSICUMS (PEPPERS)
1 SMALL ONION, FINELY CHOPPED
1 GARLIC CLOVE, FINELY CHOPPED
100 ML (3½ FL OZ) THIN (POURING) CREAM
10 BASIL LEAVES
EXTRA VIRGIN OLIVE OIL

Preheat the oven to 200°C (400°F).

Place the capsicums on a baking tray and cook in the oven for about 20 minutes until soft. Remove from the oven. When cooked, halve and remove the seeds and clean the capsicums, then coarsely chop them into pieces. Set them aside.

Heat the olive oil in a heavy-based saucepan over medium heat and cook the onion and garlic until translucent, about 3–4 minutes. Add the capsicum and cream and simmer gently until the onion and capsicum have cooked completely. This should only take around 12 minutes.

Allow the mixture to cool slightly before transferring the mixture to a food processor. Add the basil leaves, some salt and pepper and a drizzle of olive oil. Blitz until a smooth consistency is achieved.

Adjust seasoning and serve.

BUTTER & SAGE SAUCE

MAKES
150 GRAMS (5½ OZ)

THERE'S NOTHING QUITE LIKE THE SIMPLE THINGS IN LIFE, AND THIS RECIPE IS JUST THAT. INTRODUCE OTHER FAVOURITE INGREDIENTS SUCH AS SLICED MUSHROOMS, FRESH HERBS OR PANCETTA TO MAKE THIS RECIPE YOUR OWN.

150 G (5½ OZ) UNSALTED BUTTER
12 SAGE LEAVES

Melt the butter in a frying pan over medium heat and allow it to foam. Add the sage leaves and keep the butter on low bubbling heat until it starts to darken slightly in colour. Remove from the heat and serve.

SOFRITTO

MAKES
450 GRAMS (1 LB)

A SOFRITTO FORMS THE BASE OF MANY DISHES IN ITALIAN CUISINE AND IS OFTEN THE STARTING POINT FOR MOST WHITE SAUCES. A GOOD SOFRITTO CAN BECOME A WONDERFUL SAUCE IN ITS OWN RIGHT.

½ ONION, COARSELY CHOPPED
1 LARGE CARROT, COARSELY CHOPPED
2 CELERY STALKS, COARSELY CHOPPED
BOUQUET GARNI: SPRIGS OF PARSLEY, SAGE, OREGANO AND THYME
1 TABLESPOON OLIVE OIL
2 TEASPOONS BUTTER, PLUS EXTRA TO FINISH (OPTIONAL)
2 GARLIC CLOVES, CRUSHED
1 TABLESPOON TOMATO PASTE (CONCENTRATED PURÉE)
100 ML (3½ FL OZ) WHITE WINE
150 ML (5 FL OZ) CHICKEN STOCK (OR VEGETABLE IF PREFERRED), PLUS EXTRA IF NEEDED

Using a food processor, blitz separately the onion, carrot and celery. Set aside in three small bowls.

Prepare your bouquet garni by bunching your herbs and tying neatly together with kitchen string.

Heat up the olive oil and butter in a large saucepan over low heat, then add the blitzed onion and garlic. Keep the heat low and stir with a wooden spoon so as not to burn the garlic. Add a dash of salt at this stage. Now add the blitzed carrot and celery and stir.

Add the bouquet garni, tomato paste, white wine and stock, stirring gently for about a minute. Partially cover the saucepan and let the liquids reduce for 45 minutes to 1 hour, or until the sauce has reached a fairly thick and textured consistency. If the sauce is a little dry, feel free to add more stock or water as required.

Remove the bouquet garni and season to taste with salt and pepper.

Optional: Stir through a knob of butter for a little touch of decadence.

AIOLI

MAKES
300 GRAMS (10½ OZ)

THIS CLASSIC AIOLI CAN BE USED AS A DIP FOR YOUR MEATBALLS, OR IT CAN BE JAZZED UP WITH BARBECUE SAUCE OR WASABI PASTE AND MADE INTO AN AMAZING MEATBALL SAUCE.

- 2 EGG YOLKS
- 250 ML (9 FL OZ/1 CUP) OLIVE OIL
- 2 ROASTED GARLIC CLOVES, CRUSHED
- 1 TABLESPOON WHITE WINE VINEGAR
- 2 TEASPOONS WASABI PASTE (OPTIONAL)
- 2 TEASPOONS BARBECUE SAUCE (SEE OPPPOSITE) (OPTIONAL)

Add the egg yolks to a food blender and start to introduce the olive oil a little at a time to create a mayonnaise. Once all of the oil has been absorbed into the egg mixture, add the garlic and vinegar and combine thoroughly. Season to taste with salt and white pepper if desired.

Optional extra: For a different spin on this recipe, add 2 teaspoons of wasabi paste or Barbecue Sauce into the mix.

SLOW-COOKED MEAT SAUCE

MAKES
780 GRAMS (11½ OZ)

FOR THE AVID MEAT LOVER, THIS DELICIOUS, VERSATILE SAUCE IS FOR YOU. IT CAN FORM THE BASE OF A BOLOGNESE FOR PASTA, CAN BE SPREAD BETWEEN PASTA SHEETS IN LASAGNE AND, OF COURSE, CAN BE LADLED OVER YOUR FAVOURITE MEATBALLS FOR AN EVEN MEATIER EXPERIENCE.

- ½ ONION, COARSELY CHOPPED
- 1 SMALL CARROT, CHOPPED
- 1 CELERY STALK, CHOPPED
- 4 GARLIC CLOVES
- 30 G (1 OZ/1 SMALL BUNCH) FLAT-LEAF (ITALIAN) PARSLEY
- 20 G (¾ OZ/1 SMALL BUNCH) THYME
- OLIVE OIL
- 50 G (1¾ OZ) MINCED (GROUND) CHICKEN THIGH
- 50 G (1¾ OZ) MINCED (GROUND) PORK
- 150 G (5½ OZ) MINCED (GROUND) BEEF
- 170 ML (5½ FL OZ/⅔ CUP) WHITE WINE
- 400 G (14 OZ) TINNED CHOPPED TOMATOES
- 1 DRIED BAY LEAF
- 2 TEASPOONS FRESHLY GRATED NUTMEG

In a food processor, whizz up the onion, carrot, celery, garlic, parsley and thyme until finely chopped.

Heat up a good drizzle of olive oil in a large saucepan over medium heat and cook the processed vegetables for 2–3 minutes. Add a pinch of salt at this stage.

Add the chicken, pork and beef, and thoroughly stir through. The meat will start to release some liquid: continue cooking and stirring until the mixture is dry and all the moisture from the meat has evaporated. Then, the meat will start to brown at this stage. Cook for 5 minutes and then add the white wine and let it reduce until dry again.

Add the tomato, the bay leaf and nutmeg. You can also add another good drizzle of olive oil at this stage if you wish. Reduce the heat, add the lid and cook for 2 hours.

Season to taste at the end of cooking.

HOT TOMATO & EGGPLANT SAUCE

MAKES
1 KILOGRAM (2 LB 4 OZ)

THE BASE OF THIS SAUCE IS TOMATO AND EGGPLANT, TOGETHER WITH A RANGE OF FRAGRANT HERBS. THE NEXT ELEMENT TO THIS SAUCE IS HEAT, SO CHOOSE YOUR CHILLI WISELY AND YOU'LL SOON HAVE A PERFECTLY BALANCED SAUCE TO ACCOMPANY A MULTITUDE OF DISHES.

3 TABLESPOONS OLIVE OIL
1 KG (2 LB 4 OZ) FRESH RIPE TOMATOES, CHOPPED
½ BROWN ONION, COARSELY CHOPPED
1 EGGPLANT (AUBERGINE), DICED
2 GARLIC CLOVES, COARSELY CHOPPED
1 LARGE FRESH RED CHILLI, DICED
½ SMALL BUNCH FRESH OREGANO
4 ROSEMARY SPRIGS, LEAVES PICKED
2 LARGE HANDFULS BASIL, COARSELY CHOPPED
2 DRIED BAY LEAVES
300 ML (10½ FL OZ) CHICKEN STOCK
1 TEASPOON CHILLI FLAKES (MORE OR LESS TO TASTE)

Pour the olive oil into a wide heavy-based saucepan and set over high heat until smoking, then add the chopped tomatoes. Add a pinch of salt and the onion and cook, constantly stirring, until the tomatoes have broken down and the onion has partially cooked.

Reduce the heat and add the eggplant, garlic, red chilli and all of the herbs. Cover with chicken stock and continue to cook for a further 30 minutes. Mix in the chilli flakes and taste. Adjust as required.

Remove the bay leaves and allow to cool slightly before placing everything into a food processor and pulsing until a finer consistency is reached (not too smooth).

Season to taste.

BARBECUE SAUCE

MAKES
600 GRAMS (1 LB 5 OZ)

THOUGH ESSENTIALLY VERY SIMPLE, THIS WILL QUICKLY BECOME YOUR NUMBER ONE GO-TO SAUCE FOR ANY STYLE OF GRILLED MEATS. ONCE YOU HAVE MASTERED THIS RECIPE, ADJUST IT TO SUIT YOUR TASTE, MAKE IT IN BULK AND STORE IT IN THE REFRIGERATOR FOR USE OVER SEVERAL WEEKS.

1½ TABLESPOONS CANOLA OIL
60 G (2¼ OZ) ONION, FINELY DICED
5 GARLIC CLOVES, FINELY DICED
2 TABLESPOONS SMOKED PAPRIKA
1 PINCH CHILLI POWDER
1 TABLESPOON THYME LEAVES
150 ML (5 FL OZ) TOMATO SAUCE (KETCHUP)
120 G (4¼ OZ) MOLASSES
30 G (1 OZ) DIJON MUSTARD
½ TABLESPOON WORCESTERSHIRE SAUCE
230 ML (7¾ FL OZ) CIDER VINEGAR
20 G (¾ OZ) LIGHT BROWN SUGAR

Mix all the ingredients together in a bowl with a pinch of salt and 100 ml (3½ fl oz) of water. Whisk until the sugar has started to break down and everything is thoroughly combined.

RED WINE & ONION SAUCE

MAKES
250 GRAMS (9 OZ)

BEAUTIFULLY DELICATE AND VELVETY, THIS SAUCE IS SIMPLE TO MAKE. USE YOUR FAVOURITE WINE AND EXPERIMENT WITH DIFFERENT STYLES, FROM BIG FRUITY REDS TO MORE SUBDUED VARIETIES.

- OLIVE OIL
- 80 G (2¾ OZ) FRENCH SHALLOTS, FINELY DICED
- ½ SMALL CARROT (ABOUT 40 G/ 1¼ OZ), FINELY DICED
- 2 DRIED BAY LEAVES
- 4 THYME SPRIGS
- 1 ROSEMARY SPRIG
- 1 GARLIC CLOVE, SMASHED
- 400 ML (14 FL OZ) RED WINE
- 40 G (1½ OZ) UNSALTED BUTTER, CUT INTO CUBES
- JUICE OF ½ LEMON
- 30 G (1 OZ) PARMESAN CHEESE, VERY FINELY GRATED
- 1 SMALL HANDFUL FLAT-LEAF (ITALIAN) PARSLEY, FINELY CHOPPED

Heat up a good drizzle of olive oil in a saucepan over medium heat and sauté the French shallot, carrot and a pinch of salt for about 5 minutes. Add the bay leaves, thyme, rosemary and garlic and continue to cook, stirring, for about 8 minutes, until the vegetables are completely cooked.

Add a dash of the red wine, stirring for 30 seconds to deglaze the pan, then pour in the remaining wine and bring to the boil. Reduce the heat and cook the sauce at a gentle simmer for about 12 minutes, or until all of the alcohol has been cooked out of the wine. (Smelling the cooking vapour will let you know if there's still alcohol left.)

Pick out the herbs and garlic. Introduce small cubes of butter into the sauce one at a time, stirring vigorously each time until fully dissolved. Continue until all the butter has been incorporated. Add the lemon juice and a good crank of black pepper. Remove the sauce from the heat and whisk in the parmesan cheese. Finish by stirring through the parsley.

Serve while hot.

HORSERADISH CREAM

MAKES
325 GRAMS (11½ OZ)

HERE'S A SIMPLE SAUCE WITH SOME SERIOUS KICK. ONCE YOU'VE TESTED THIS RECIPE, ADJUST THE AMOUNT OF GRATED HORSERADISH TO SUIT YOUR TASTE. THIS STYLE OF SAUCE WORKS PERFECTLY WITH MOST MEATS, BUT PARTICULARLY RED MEATS.

- 150 ML (5 FL OZ) THICKENED (WHIPPING) CREAM
- 150 ML (5 FL OZ) MAYONNAISE
- 25 G (1 OZ/¼ CUP) FRESHLY GRATED HORSERADISH

Whip the cream in a mixing bowl until soft peaks form, then gently fold through the mayonnaise. Add fresh horseradish and fold through. Finish with a pinch of salt and a good grind of black pepper.

RED WINE & BEEF STOCK SAUCE

MAKES
600 GRAMS (1 LB 5 OZ)

A RED WINE SAUCE CAN BE MADE EVEN BETTER BY ADDING THE RESIDUAL COOKING JUICES LEFT OVER FROM BAKING MEATBALLS IN THE OVEN. THIS RECIPE TAKES THE IDEA ONE STEP FURTHER BY COMBINING YOUR FAVOURITE RED WINE AND GOOD-QUALITY BEEF STOCK WITH VEGETABLES TO FORM A FLAVOURSOME, RICH SAUCE, WHICH WORKS PERFECTLY WITH ALMOST ALL BEEF MEATBALL RECIPES.

2–3 TABLESPOONS OLIVE OIL
2 DRIED BAY LEAVES
½ BROWN ONION, SKIN ON, COARSELY CHOPPED
½ CARROT, SKIN ON, COARSELY CHOPPED
1 CELERY STALK, COARSELY CHOPPED
1 GARLIC CLOVE, SMASHED
500 ML (17 FL OZ/2 CUPS) RED WINE
300 ML (10½ FL OZ) BEEF STOCK
1 TABLESPOON TOMATO PASTE (CONCENTRATED PURÉE)
20 G (¾ OZ) BUTTER
2 TEASPOONS FINELY GRATED PARMESAN CHEESE
2 HANDFULS FLAT-LEAF (ITALIAN) PARSLEY, FINELY CHOPPED
JUICE OF ¼ ORANGE

Start by heating up a good amount of olive oil in a heavy-based saucepan over medium heat. Add the bay leaves and chopped vegetables (you can leave the skins on the onion and garlic, and no need to peel the carrot). Add a pinch of salt and stir.

Brown the vegetables for several minutes, then add the red wine and the beef stock. Stir in the tomato paste and turn down the heat, simmering for at least 45 minutes. Strain the liquid through a sieve and return to the pan.

Whisk in the butter and the parmesan cheese, and allow the sauce to reduce by half. Add the parsley and the orange juice, and drizzle some olive oil over the top. Season to taste.

SPICY HOISIN SAUCE WITH GINGER & GARLIC

MAKES
200 GRAMS (7 OZ)

A HIGHLY AROMATIC ASIAN-STYLE SAUCE, THIS GOES PERFECTLY WITH THE ASIAN-INSPIRED MEATBALL RECIPES, SUCH AS PORK, PEANUT & WATER CHESTNUT (P 70) AND PORK, BEEF & GINGER (P 68). IT CAN BE USED AS A DIPPING SAUCE OR CAN BE DRIZZLED OVER THE FINAL DISH.

2 TEASPOONS SOY SAUCE
2 TABLESPOONS SESAME OIL
80 ML (2½ FL OZ/⅓ CUP) RICE VINEGAR
2 TABLESPOONS MIRIN (RICE WINE)
80 ML (2½ FL OZ/⅓ CUP) HOISIN SAUCE
2 TEASPOONS HONEY
2 TEASPOONS FINELY GRATED GINGER
1 GARLIC CLOVE, FINELY GRATED
1 TABLESPOON SRIRACHA CHILLI SAUCE

Mix all of the ingredients together until fully combined.

CREAMY MUSHROOM SAUCE

MAKES
700 GRAMS (1 LB 9 OZ)

A COMBINATION OF FRESH SWISS BROWN MUSHROOMS AS WELL AS DRIED PORCINI MUSHROOMS IS USED IN THIS WONDERFUL MUSHROOM SAUCE. IT WORKS INCREDIBLY WELL WITH ANY STYLE OF MEAT, ESPECIALLY BEEF. THE ADDITION OF THE ORANGE ZEST BRIGHTENS THE SAUCE AND HELPS TO BALANCE AND CUT THROUGH THE CREAM.

- 50 G (1¾ OZ) DRIED PORCINI MUSHROOMS
- 30 G (1 OZ) UNSALTED BUTTER
- OLIVE OIL
- ½ BROWN ONION
- 300 G (10½ OZ) SWISS BROWN MUSHROOMS, SLICED
- 1 GARLIC CLOVE
- 6 SAGE LEAVES
- 125 ML (4 FL OZ/½ CUP) DRY WHITE WINE
- 300 ML (10½ FL OZ) THIN (POURING) CREAM
- 25 G (1 OZ/¼ CUP) FINELY GRATED PARMESAN CHEESE
- ZEST OF ¼ ORANGE

Soak the dried porcini mushrooms in the warm water until they become soft. Reserve the residual liquid and strain it through a fine strainer to remove any fine particles.

Heat up the butter and a drizzle of olive oil in a saucepan over medium heat, then add the onion and cook until translucent, about 3–4 minutes. Add the Swiss brown mushrooms, garlic and sage, and cook over low heat until the mushrooms become tender.

Add the wine and bring to the boil, then reduce the heat and stir in the cream. Add the porcini mushrooms and some of the residual water. Let the sauce simmer until a nice, rich consistency is achieved.

Add the parmesan cheese and the orange zest, and stir through. Season with salt and pepper to taste.

GREEN SAUCE

MAKES
280 GRAMS (10 OZ)

NOT A PESTO AND NOT A SALSA VERDE, THIS RECIPE IS A COMBINATION OF BOTH AND IS WONDERFULLY FRESH AND FLAVOURSOME. IT WORKS PERFECTLY WITH ALL MEATS, VEGETABLES AND FISH.

- 50 G (1¾ OZ/1 LARGE BUNCH) FLAT-LEAF (ITALIAN) PARSLEY, LEAVES PICKED
- 50 G (1¾ OZ/1 LARGE BUNCH) BASIL, LEAVES PICKED
- 1 GARLIC CLOVE
- 35 G (1¼ OZ) ALMONDS
- 10 G (¼ OZ) ANCHOVIES
- JUICE OF 1 LEMON
- 120 ML (4 FL OZ/½ CUP) EXTRA VIRGIN OLIVE OIL
- 25 G (1 OZ/¼ CUP) FINELY GRATED PARMESAN CHEESE

Blitz the herbs, garlic, almonds, anchovies, lemon juice, olive oil and a pinch of salt and pepper in a food processor. This should only take a minute. Once a smooth sauce has formed, add the parmesan cheese and blitz for another minute.

NAPOLI CRUDA (UNCOOKED NAPOLI SAUCE)

MAKES
1 KILOGRAM (2 LB 4 OZ)

AN INCREDIBLY FRAGRANT CLASSIC SAUCE, THE NAPOLI CRUDA CAN BE STORED IN THE REFRIGERATOR AND USED FOR ALL TYPES OF MEATBALLS. IT'S BEST SERVED COOL OR AT ROOM TEMPERATURE, AND RELIES UPON THE RIPENESS OF YOUR TOMATOES AND THE QUALITY OF YOUR OLIVE OIL.

- 1 KG (2 LB 4 OZ) RIPE TOMATOES
- 100 G (3½ OZ) GREEN AND BLACK OLIVES, PITTED AND SLICED
- 30 G (1 OZ/1 SMALL BUNCH) BASIL LEAVES, TORN
- 2 FRESH OREGANO SPRIGS, LEAVES PICKED AND CHOPPED
- EXTRA VIRGIN OLIVE OIL
- JUICE OF ½ A LEMON
- 1 WHITE ANCHOVY, CHOPPED (OPTIONAL)

Remove the skin from your ripened tomatoes by scoring the tomato with a knife, then dropping them into boiling water for 1 minute. The skin should peel off easily. Chop the tomatoes and set them aside in a strainer to drain for at least 1 hour.

Combine the olives, basil, oregano and tomato. Add a drizzle of extra virgin olive oil and season with salt and pepper to taste, adjusting with a squeeze of lemon juice if required. Add a white anchovy for more flavour.

Note: White anchovies are far less salty and much lighter in flavour (and in colour) than common anchovies due to being pickled in vinegar.

SEAFOOD BISQUE

MAKES
650 GRAMS (1 LB 7 OZ)

SEAFOOD BISQUE IS A RATHER INDULGENT DISH, AND THIS VERSION IS NO EXCEPTION. IT ALSO DOUBLES AS AN INCREDIBLE SAUCE FOR MOST SEAFOOD-BASED BALLS.

- 2½ TABLESPOONS OLIVE OIL
- CRUSTACEAN SHELLS – LOBSTER, PRAWNS (SHRIMP), CRAB – AS MANY AS YOU CAN GET
- 1 ONION, COARSELY CHOPPED
- 1 CELERY STALK, DICED
- 1 CARROT, COARSELY CHOPPED
- 100 G (3½ OZ) TOMATO PASTE (CONCENTRATED PURÉE)
- 4 THYME SPRIGS, COARSELY CHOPPED
- 1 DRIED BAY LEAF
- ZEST OF ¼ ORANGE
- 1 LITRE (35 FL OZ/4 CUPS) VEGETABLE STOCK
- 2 SHOTS RICARD PASTIS, OR OTHER ANISE-FLAVOURED LIQUEUR
- 200 ML (7 FL OZ) THIN (POURING) CREAM

Pour the olive oil into a stockpot over medium–high heat. When the oil is hot, add the shells and cook until they are roasted and take on a darker colour. This should take 6–8 minutes. Remove the shells and set them aside.

In the same pot, add the vegetables and cook until they take on some nice colour, about 10 minutes. Add the tomato paste and cook for 2–3 minutes. Return the shells to the pot and add the herbs and the orange zest. Cover with stock and Ricard pastis and gently simmer over low heat for 1 hour.

Allow the sauce to cool slightly before putting everything through a heavy-duty food processor, then pass the mixture through a coarse strainer and then a fine chinois, gauze or sieve.

Place the sauce back into the pot over low heat and reduce by one-third. Stir in the cream. Allow the sauce to cool slightly, then blitz the mixture again and pass it through a fine chinois one more time before serving.

Parmesan crisps

Here's an interesting way to add texture to any dish. Bake parmesan cheese in thin sheets – it crisps up into delectable wafers, which can be broken into pieces for texture or carefully positioned on your plate for visual effect.

45 G (1½ OZ/½ CUP) COARSELY CHOPPED PARMESAN CHEESE

Preheat the oven to 165°C (320°F).

Place a heaped tablespoon of parmesan onto a silicone baking sheet and lightly pat down. (Alternatively, use baking paper on a tray.) Repeat with the remaining parmesan, keeping at least 5 cm (2 in) distance between each tablespoon portion. Bake for 12–15 minutes, or until crispy.

Remove from the oven and transfer to a cutting board where you can cut the cheese into any shape you desire. Set the parmesan shapes aside to cool. The parmesan crisps retain all their wonderful saltiness and bring a textural element to any dish.

Toasted pistachios

Highly addictive, toasted pistachios make a great addition to any dish that requires some extra crunch. Experiment with the coarseness of the nut by crushing the pistachios after baking, or leave them whole for full effect.

100 G (3½ OZ) PISTACHIO NUT KERNELS

Preheat the oven to 100°C (200°F).

Spread the pistachios out on a baking tray and bake in the oven for 10 minutes. The toasted pistachios will soon darken in colour and become a little firmer, and they'll continue to harden as they cool.

Fried sage

These fried sage leaves are incredibly delicate and can be a subtle way of garnishing a dish to add an additional textural element and the savoury notes of cooked herbs.

40 SAGE LEAVES
OLIVE OIL, FOR COATING

Preheat the oven to 180°C (350°F).

Toss the sage leaves in a little olive oil to coat. Arrange on a baking tray. Bake in the oven for around 6 minutes. Remove from the oven and set aside to cool. Garnish by scattering them over the top before serving.

Micro herbs

Increasingly popular, these tiny leaves enliven a dish with their vibrant colour, and can also bring a welcome freshness to a meal. Available at most good grocers, micro herbs of all varieties work incredibly well as a garnish. Once washed, simply pick or cut the micro herbs (you can use the entire stem) and sprinkle them over the finished dish.

Herb oil

Personalise your garnish by adding your favourite herbs and letting them infuse into some good-quality olive oil. If using soft herbs like basil or parsley, wash them thoroughly and blanch them for 20 seconds in boiling water. This will assist in keeping the herb colour vibrant in the oil.

Edible flowers

Available at fresh grocery stores, edible flowers add an interesting visual element when garnishing a dish. Although they don't rate very highly on the flavour scale, their vibrancy and colour certainly register and when used with a delicate hand, can really brighten up even the dullest of dishes.

Chilli oil

For those who love having a chilli hit at the ready at all times, this is the ideal oil to make and keep stored away until your next meatball feast. This recipe is for approximately 1 litre (35 fl oz/4 cups) of chilli oil – plenty to keep you going or to transfer to small vessels to give away as gifts.

1 LITRE (35 FL OZ/4 CUPS) OLIVE OIL
½ BUNCH THYME
120 G (4¼ OZ) BIRD'S EYE CHILLI, THICKLY SLICED
1 LEMON, HALVED
25 G (1 OZ) GARLIC (ABOUT 5 CLOVES), CRUSHED
1 TABLESPOON WHOLE BLACK PEPPERCORNS
110 G (3¾ OZ) CHILLI FLAKES

Pour the olive oil into a deep heavy-set saucepan over medium–high heat and add the thyme, sliced chilli, lemon, garlic, peppercorns and 1 tablespoon of salt. Bring the mixture to the boil. Once it's bubbling nicely, reduce the heat and simmer for 15 minutes. Now, add the chilli flakes and cook for another 10 minutes.

Remove the oil from the heat and allow to cool completely. Once cooled, pass the entire mixture through a superfine strainer or muslin cloth.

Truffle salt

High-quality truffle salt can be expensive, but a little goes a long way. Try seasoning your dish with a pinch of truffle salt to unlock deep, earthy flavour notes. Truffle salt works amazingly well with almost all meats and almost all of the sotto palle mentioned in this book.

Fresh herbs

There's nothing quite like freshly picked herbs to liven up a meatball dish. Torn by hand or roughly chopped with a sharp knife, herbs like flat-leaf (Italian) parsley, mint, dill, oregano, coriander (cilantro), tarragon and rosemary are all wonderful contributors to a meal.

Salt flakes

Salt flakes, as opposed to regular granulated table salt, has a more gentle level of saltiness due to lower sodium levels. This results in a more subtle salt hit, which is exactly what you need when finishing a dish. Crack the salt flakes between your fingers as you garnish a dish and apply liberally.

Citrus zest

The zest of oranges, lemons and limes is a quick, way to add vibrancy to your meatballs via delicate acidity, cutting through the richness of the meat and helping to cleanse the palate, ready for your next mouthful. Always keep some citrus fruit handy to finely grate over your meatballs.

Prosciutto crisps

Wonderfully crunchy, prosciutto crisps add a layer of salty goodness to your favourite meatball dish. Arrange some thinly sliced prosciutto on baking paper and bake in a 180°C (350°F) oven for around 8 minutes, or until the prosciutto goes crispy.

Grated cheese

The king of all grated cheeses has to be aged Parmigiano Reggiano. Wallet permitting, ask for the highest-quality parmesan you can find and you'll be rewarded with a deep, rich flavour delivered by the ever-present umami found in abundance in aged parmesan cheese.

Cracked black pepper

Pepper is fairly commonplace when it comes to seasoning a dish, but buying fresh black peppercorns and cracking them coarsely over your meatballs at the last moment unlocks the complex and distinctive flavour of black pepper. Try using white peppercorns, finely cracked over meatballs or sauces for an even hotter peppery experience.

Thinly sliced apple

Adding crunch and freshness to your meatballs, thinly sliced apple not only looks appealing, but gives the finished dish some colour and vibrancy. Leave the skin on different coloured apples for visual effect and experiment with different shapes and sizes, whether it be slices, matchsticks or finely diced pieces of apple.

Flavoured butter

Trick up your favourite butter with a variety of herbs, spices and other ingredients to bring another layer of flavour to your meatball dish. Coarsely chop fresh herbs such as sage, oregano and rosemary, or use some finely grated citrus zest or flavoured salts, and mix thoroughly through room temperature salted butter. Roll the flavoured butter into a log, wrap tightly in plastic wrap and store in the fridge or freezer. Slice off the amount you need at the last minute to finish a host of dishes.

Pickled zucchini

Pickled zucchini brings a bright acidic freshness to any dish and works perfectly to cut through fatty meats. Make these in large batches and store in the fridge, or package them nicely for the perfect gift.

1 KG (2 LB 4 OZ) ZUCCHINI (COURGETTES), THINLY SLICED (TO 2 MM)
250 ML (9 FL OZ/1 CUP) WHITE WINE VINEGAR
220 G (7¾ OZ/1 CUP) SUGAR
1 TEASPOON YELLOW MUSTARD SEEDS
1 TEASPOON CELERY SEEDS
1 TEASPOON TUMERIC POWDER

Place the zucchini in a colander and combine gently with 1 teaspoon of salt. Let the colander stand in a bowl for 2 hours, then rinse well and pat dry with a tea towel (dish towel).

Mix the vinegar, sugar, spices and 2 tablespoons of salt in a saucepan and bring to the boil, then simmer for 5 minutes. Remove from the heat and let the mixture cool slightly, before adding the zucchini.

Leave in the refrigerator overnight to marinate in the pickling liquid. Drain the zucchini, making sure to save the pickling juice. Transfer the zucchini to sterilised jars and cover with the reserved pickling juice. Store in the refrigerator and serve as required. The zucchini can be stored in the pickling juice in the refrigerator for around 2 weeks.

Prawn oil

This infused oil takes on the deep flavour of toasted prawn and works incredibly well with any of the seafood fish balls. Keep this oil in the refrigerator and enjoy it with seafood and pasta, or be surprised at how well it works with meats, especially beef.

500 ML (17 FL OZ/2 CUPS) OLIVE OIL
20 PRAWN (SHRIMP) HEADS
ZEST OF ½ ORANGE
1 TEASPOON CHILLI FLAKES
2 FRESH BAY LEAVES
1 TABLESPOON WHOLE BLACK PEPPERCORNS

Pour a small drizzle of olive oil into a saucepan and set over medium heat until brought up to temperature. Add the prawn heads with a pinch of salt. Using a wooden spoon, smash the shells so they break up into small pieces. Regulate the temperature of the saucepan so as not to burn the shells. Cook for 5 minutes.

Add the orange zest, chilli flakes, bay leaves and peppercorns, and stir through for 2–3 minutes. Reduce the heat to low. Add the rest of the olive oil and allow to cook very gently for 30 minutes. The oil should not go above 60°C (140°F).

Take the saucepan off the heat. The residual heat in the saucepan will assist with infusing the flavour of the prawns into the oil. Allow this to cool completely before passing all of the oil through fine gauze and into a serving vessel. Keep the oil in the refrigerator and use liberally.

Hazelnut pangrattato

A moreish garnish, this nutty herbed breadcrumb mixture delivers added texture and flavour to your meatball dish. Keep it in the refrigerator and use it on top of not only meatballs, but also on fish and soft cheeses like mozzarella.

40 G (1½ OZ) BUTTER
1 GARLIC CLOVE, FINELY CHOPPED
100 G (3½ OZ) DRY BREADCRUMBS
SALT FLAKES
3 TABLESPOONS FINELY CHOPPED SAGE LEAVES
1 TABLESPOON HAZELNUTS, ROASTED, SKINNED AND CRUSHED MEDIUM-FINE
2 TABLESPOONS CHOPPED FLAT-LEAF (ITALIAN) PARSLEY
ZEST OF 1 LEMON

Add the butter to a saucepan and bring to a gentle foam over medium heat. Add the garlic, breadcrumbs and some salt flakes, and stir until golden brown. Then add the sage and hazelnuts and stir for 1 minute. Remove from the heat and allow to cool, then stir through the parsley and lemon zest.

Fresh red chilli

Add heat to your meatballs by thinly slicing some fresh red chillies and sprinkling them over your finished dish. To experience the full potential of your chilli, leave in the seeds, but be sure to warn your guests. For more subtle heat, remove the inner white membrane and seeds before slicing.

INDEX

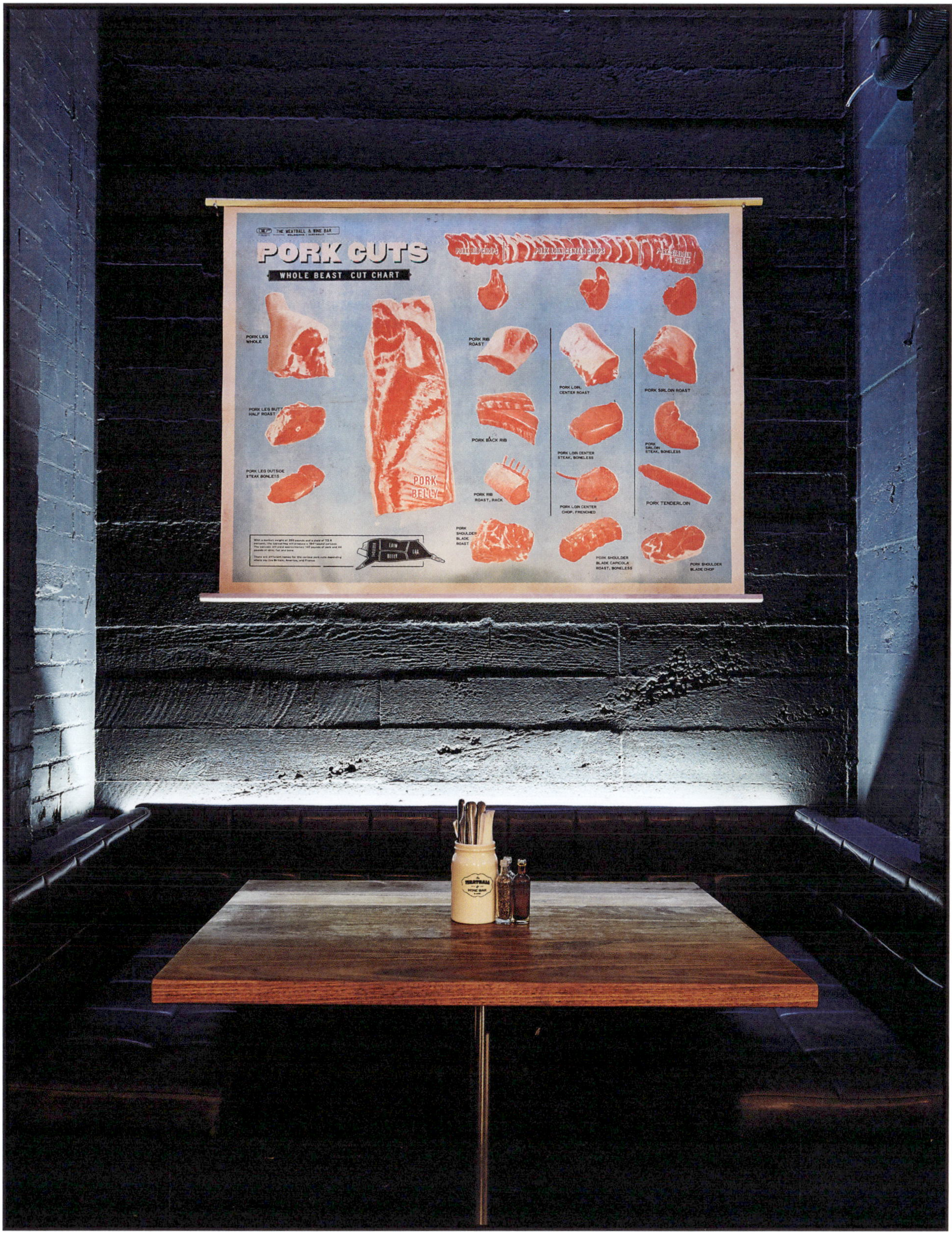
THE MEATBALL & WINE BAR
PORK CUTS
WHOLE BEAST CUT CHART
PORK RIB CHOPS
PORK LOIN CENTER CHOPS
PORK SIRLOIN CHOPS
PORK LEG WHOLE
PORK RIB ROAST
PORK LOIN, CENTER ROAST
PORK SIRLOIN ROAST
PORK LEG BUTT HALF ROAST
PORK BACK RIB
PORK LOIN CENTER STEAK, BONELESS
PORK SIRLOIN STEAK, BONELESS
PORK LEG OUTSIDE STEAK BONLESS
PORK BELLY
PORK RIB ROAST, RACK
PORK LOIN CENTER CHOP, FRENCHED
PORK TENDERLOIN
PORK SHOULDER BLADE ROAST
PORK SHOULDER BLADE CAPICOLA ROAST, BONELESS
PORK SHOULDER BLADE CHOP
LOIN
BELLY
LEG

Acknowledgments

A very special thanks: to my parents, Arcella and Valter Bruno, and my three brothers, Renato, Fabrizio and Davide, for their ongoing love and support. To my girl Alice for being my official taste tester and Hero for eating all of the leftovers. To Terry Durack and Jill Dupleix for coming up with the fabulous idea for this book. To Guy Salmon for working tirelessly during the shoot and Simmer Kahlon for keeping the restaurants under control. To Alicia Taylor for taking such amazing photographs and Deborah Kaloper for making my meatballs look so tasty. To Susie Ashworth for wading through all of my notes and Aileen Lord for the great design. To Sue Hines, Corinne Roberts, Barbara McClenahan and Vivien Valk from Murdoch Books for being so easy to work with and making all of this possible. To Stefano de Pieri, Guy Grossi, Jane Lawson, Pete Evans, Neil Perry, Katrina Pizzini, Mario and Adam for their contributions. And, of course, to all the MBWB crew – past, present and future.

First published as *Meatballs* in 2015 by Murdoch Books, an imprint of Allen & Unwin.
This edition published in 2021.

Murdoch Books Australia
83 Alexander Street
Crows Nest NSW 2065
Phone: +61 (0) 2 8425 0100
Fax: +61 (0) 2 9906 2218
murdochbooks.com.au
info@murdochbooks.com.au

Murdoch Books UK
Ormond House
26-27 Boswell Street
London WC1N 3JZ
Phone: +44 (0) 20 8785 5995
murdochbooks.co.uk
info@murdochbooks.co.uk

For corporate orders and custom publishing, contact our business development team at salesenquiries@murdochbooks.com.au

Publisher: Corinne Roberts
Editorial Manager: Barbara McClenahan
Design Manager: Vivien Valk
Project Editor: Susie Ashworth
Internal Designer: Aileen Lord
Cover Designer: Madeleine Kane
Photographer: Alicia Taylor
Stylist: Deborah Kaloper
Production Manager: Mary Bjelobrk

A catalogue record for this book is available from the National Library of Australia

ISBN 978 1 92235 147 0 Australia

Colour reproduction by Splitting Image Colour Studio Pty Ltd, Clayton, Victoria
Printed by C & C Offset Printing Co. Ltd., China

10 9 8 7 6 5 4 3 2 1

The paper in this book is FSC® certified. FSC® promotes environmentally responsible, socially beneficial and economically viable management of the world's forests.

IMPORTANT: Those who might be at risk from the effects of salmonella poisoning (the elderly, pregnant women, young children and those suffering from immune deficiency diseases) should consult their doctor with any concerns about eating raw eggs. Please ensure that all seafood and beef to be eaten raw or lightly cooked are very fresh and of the highest quality.

OVEN GUIDE: You may find cooking times vary depending on the oven you are using. For fan-forced ovens, as a general rule, set the oven temperature to 20°C (35°F) lower than indicated in the recipe.

MEASURES GUIDE: We have used 20 ml (4 teaspoon) tablespoon measures. If you are using a 15 ml (3 teaspoon) tablespoon add an extra teaspoon of the ingredient for each tablespoon specified.